INVEST
AND GROW RICH!

FIVE
UNIVERSAL
RULES FOR
UNLIMITED
WEALTH
CREATION

▼

J. RICHARD CHARLTON
with DAVID SINGH

Published in 1997 by
McLeod Publishing

Distributed in Canada by
General Distribution Services Inc.
30 Lesmill Road
Toronto, Canada M3B 2T6
Tel. (416) 445-3333
Fax (416) 445-5967
E-mail Customer.Service@ccmailgw.genpub.com

Distributed in the United States by
General Distribution Services Inc.
85 River Rock Drive, Suite 202
Buffalo, New York 14207
Toll-free Tel. 1-800-805-1083
Toll-free Fax 1-800-481-6207
E-mail gdsinc@genpub.com

01 00 99 98   3 4 5

ISBN 0-919292-046

CIP data available from the National Library of Canada

Cover design: Pekoe Jones
Design and typesetting: Kinetics Design & Illustration

Printed and bound in Canada

Contents

Preface

IN the spring of 1997, the big news was the imminent, much feared stock market correction. Many credible news sources featured market timing articles extolling the great prowess of the "seers." The writers of monthly market timing letters, analysts, and other crystal ball gazers adeptly advised the timely removal of cash from the stock market to avoid the devastation and erosion of capital that come from a correction.

By summer, the operative word of all those naysayers was a great big "oops!" The newspaper editors paid to write the world is coming to an end headlines had to write this instead: DOW SURGES PAST 8,000. And *The Wall Street Journal* quoted Michael Metz, "the perennially bearish chief investment strategist at Oppenheimer & Co.," as saying, "It's not been a happy experience, no question about it. I've been absolutely wrong about the duration and extent of the bull market. And it's embarrassing." The paper went on to say, "Hey, we all make mistakes. Waiters spill food on customers. Cab drivers lose their way. But make too many mistakes and most working stiffs lose their jobs. In the never-never land of Wall Street, though, strategists who repeatedly send investors off in the wrong direction can continue to draw salaries of $500,000 or a million bucks from brokerage firms."

But what were my clients and I doing during this scenario? We remained fully invested and rode the downturn, which turned out to be not much of a correction. And we're reaping the benefits today while others wipe the egg off their faces.

Here's what I've been saying all along: Market timing, especially in this market, is the biggest exercise in futility, because the biggest risk of the market is being out of it on the best performing days.

The lesson is quite simple. The common thread behind the phenomenal success of Warren Buffet's Berkshire Hathaway (1965 — $12/share; 1997 — $47,800/share and climbing) and Infinity Funds in the past six months is that there was no trading, no timing, just time in. Extraordinary businesses behind the stocks were simply being held for the long run.

Everyone seems to like warnings, so here's mine: Live by the headlines, die by the headlines. Rather, what you should be doing is to turn off the stock market and invest in successful businesses. Then you simply hold on through the ups and downs. Avoid the never-never land of Wall Street and Bay Street.

This book is about *growing* rich. Not *playing* the market or *risking* your life's savings. It is about making sensible decisions to begin with, and then watching the good effects of those decisions over the long term. In the pages that follow I tell you of my own pilgrimage to this approach, but I mostly give you blow-by-blow, concrete advice in how you can prepare for a very happy and secure future.

It may not be as spectacular as the doom and gloom headlines, but it's pretty exciting all the same, don't you agree?

*   *   *

This book is dedicated to the memory of my greatest mentor, my father. I would like to thank all those whose intellectual generosity has shaped my career.

RICHARD CHARLTON
Oakville, Ontario

Some Extremely Relevant Quotations

It is a gloomy moment in the history of our country. The domestic economic situation is in chaos. Our dollar is weak throughout the world. Prices are so high as to be utterly impossible. The political cauldron seethes and bubbles with uncertainty. Russia hangs as usual, like a cloud, dark and silent, upon the horizon. It is a solemn moment. Of our troubles, no man can see the end.

The Investment Letter, *Harper's Magazine*, 1847

Thirty years ago, no one could have foreseen the huge expansion of the Vietnam war, wage and price control, two oil shocks, the resignation of a president, the dissolution of the Soviet Union, a one-day drop in the Dow of 508 points, or treasury bills fluctuating between 2.8% and 17.4%. But, surprise — none of these events made the slightest dent in Ben Graham's investment principles. Nor did they render unsound the negotiated purchases of fine businesses at sensible prices. Imagine the cost to us, then, if we had let fear of unknowns cause us to defer or alter the deployment of capital. Indeed, we have usually made our best purchases when apprehensions about some macro event were at a peak. Fear is the foe of the faddist, but the friend to the fundamentalist. A different set of major shocks is sure to occur in the next 30 years. We will neither try to predict these nor profit from them. If we can identify businesses similar to those we have purchased in the past, external surprises will have little effect on our long-term results.

WARREN BUFFETT,
the world's most successful investor,
writing nearly 150 years later

Introduction

SINCE 90% of all investment advice given out today is like a bad, even pathetic, joke ("Be sure to put money every year into your RRSP!" "Buy low and sell high!" "Invest in a house as soon as possible!" "Use asset allocation!" "Sector rotation is the way to go!"), I thought I might begin this book with a favourite joke of my own:

An exceedingly wealthy Canadian has decided to throw a summer party at his palatial home in Vancouver, inviting hundreds of guests into his giant backyard. As they mill about his Olympic-sized pool, the man steps forward and makes a strange announcement:

"I have decided to hold a contest tonight. As many of you have noticed, I have filled my swimming pool with giant sharks. I here offer the choice of two glorious prizes — the hand of my beautiful daughter in marriage, or one million dollars, to whoever can swim the length of the pool and survive!"

The giant crowd gasps, and looks about at one another. True, his daughter is a wonderful catch, and a million dollars is a great offer — but what chance would any of them have to get across that shark-infested swimming pool?

The minutes tick by, and not a single person comes forward to try to claim one or the other of the fabulous prizes.

Suddenly, there is a giant splash as a young man is seen in the water, swimming furiously across the pool. After an agonizing minute or two, the fellow drags himself out of the pool on the other side, with the sharks nipping at the heels of his water-logged shoes.

"That was extraordinary!" exclaims the host. "I truly didn't think that anyone would dare to do it! Which do you want — the hand of my lovely daughter, or the one million dollars?"

The hero shakes water out of his ears and clothes and screams, "I want the sonovabitch who pushed me into the pool!"

The moral is clear: We are *all* in that pool, and for our entire lives, for it is the pool of human existence. And what are the sharks? They are inflation. Taxes. Bad advice. And most of all, they are ignorance: the ignorance that nearly all of us suffer from, that prevents us from preparing ourselves financially for our retirement years. To continue the pool analogy — the sharks are the accumulated ignorance that frightens us away from reaching "the other side" that we all desire so fervently: wealth, security, and happiness.

Ignorance is all around us, much like the weather: What is the difference between investing and gambling in mutual funds and stocks? Can we ever truly realize the vital importance of understanding the benefits of compound interest and capital growth? Isn't it risky to sell my GICs and Canada

Savings Bonds and invest that "secure money" in mutual funds or a portfolio of publicly-traded securities? Isn't it dangerous to borrow money and risk it in any kind of investments that can fluctuate greatly?

One need not be poor or under-employed to be ignorant of these issues: I have had the presidents and chairpersons of billion-dollar companies as clients, who were as ignorant of the proper way to invest as anyone else; these men were capable of running giant corporations skillfully but did not know how to handle their own money.

There are doctors who can diagnose and treat diseases with the utmost skill, but when it comes to the stock market, they melt like a snowman in July. There are lawyers who can deal with the most complex court case and argue the most arcane legal point, yet become bumbling idiots when faced with any serious investment decision.

One of my biggest complaints about our society and our school system is that almost nothing prepares us, as young boys and girls, for our financial future. Millions graduate from grade school, even high school, lacking any knowledge of the word "mortgage," much less the meaning of compound interest, or the importance of borrowing to invest. (Or the foolishness of sinking hundreds of thousands of dollars into that mortgage, for that matter.) Millions enter university without knowing about registered savings plans (and their innate flaws). Indeed, little is taught in our schools to prepare us to manage sufficiently the vast sums of money we will all earn over our respective lifetimes at our chosen professions.

My purpose in writing this book is to help countless Canadians to prepare for their retirement years — and long before — through creating and managing wealth. Yet perhaps surprisingly, this is *not* a case of easier said than done. I will show throughout this book that through simple, proven laws, which have all stood the test of time, one can ignore the irrational, greedy self-destructiveness of most investors and "stock market players." (And "playing," I can assure you, is precisely what they are doing. Playing with their money and their future, and far more often than not, they are gambling it away.)

I am a firm believer that I am in the most valuable profession in the world — and, inarguably, one of the fastest growing: wealth management and financial planning.

What makes it so worthwhile? Well, most people make money at the expense of others: the accountant earns his living by handling another's books; the pharmacist earns her living by filling someone else's prescriptions, and so on.

I have become one of Canada's most successful investment advisors because I have managed to make hundreds upon hundreds of people wealthy! I think of one client of mine who invested some $300,000 through me several years ago. Today, his portfolio is worth over $2 million. This man can now retire, due to my financial advice — and how many people can say that about any other person in their life?

My friend and mentor Nick Murray once put it quite bluntly: "We in the financial industry are the most valuable people in our clients' lives! We are even more important than their doctors!"

Is this extreme? Well, every doctor will ultimately lose his or her patients; they will all die. But when one accumulates wealth — and that's my job, in my career and in this book — that wealth will live on for decades and transcend generations!

So, I do not personally see myself as a "mutual funds

salesman" or as a "stock broker." Far from it. I am here to affect people's lives, to make a positive, welcome difference in both their futures and the futures of their children and grandchildren.

No, you *won't* get rich quick. I'll leave that for the penny-stock promoters and the people who sell lottery tickets. A handful of them will get rich, all right, but 98% will lose their wallets, if not their pants.

But if you follow the advice I shall be sharing with you over the rest of this book, in both words and charts, in all probability you cannot go wrong.

Better than that: you will make it successfully across that shark-infested pool of life, because no one will push you in or lead you astray. You'll be protected from all the dangers that surround you, because you will possess the precious knowledge of permanent-value investing, which is so simple a concept, it's almost embarrassing.

How simple? Read on . . .

1

From Insurance to
Mutual Funds

L IKE other readers of this book who have also taken many years to "find themselves," I did not come upon the selling of mutual funds as my first occupation; indeed, like a large percentage of present citizens of this country, Canada was not my first home, either!

I was born in Jamaica in 1950 to a mulatto father and a Sephardic-Jewish mother, which meant that I was considered a white man on that large Caribbean island. I was discriminated against in school, and did not enjoy high school at all. In retrospect, I was much like so many bright but restless students who see no practical use to what they are being taught in school, so I dropped out before I was 17.

I next entered an art class, and then helped my father run some hotels in Montego Bay. I'm not sure I was much help to him, but I certainly had a wonderful time, spending endless summers in one of the great resort areas of the world!

Then, when my father sold his hotel, I went to work for him at Federal Casualty Jamaica Ltd. Insurance, a company that he had founded. My dad was one of the truly great insurance men of his time, since he viewed that concept in a profound and thoughtful way.

He saw insurance as not something one buys but as a grand facility provided for the public by financial organizations, whereby one could pay them to take over, and carry out, financial obligations that each of us could not fulfill ourselves.

Maybe this was simply another way of selling insurance, but my father did provide for me — as I later took on a career in life insurance when I first came to Canada — an excellent basis for my knowledge; it was all that I knew about the industry.

My father proved to me that one could not merely use a purchase agreement form to buy a life insurance policy; one had to apply to an insurance company to obtain that policy. And so, throughout my brief career in the insurance world, I had phenomenal success, because my dad taught me that I was helping people to apply to these financial institutions to help them do things they couldn't do themselves — whether it was to fund a partnership, or feed their family if they did not make it safely home.

My dad also pointed out to me that one of the most certain, honourable things in financial planning is adequate life insurance — by setting up a financial contract to allow the insurance company to take over those responsibilities one might not, one day, be able to handle on one's own.

He dramatized for me how much debt a young family man is forced to undertake in this society — whether for a car, a house, or merely furniture. He showed me how, when a person dies, the banks and trust companies have no problem with repossessing it all, if those debts are not paid off.

Ahh, but they will never repossess your wife and children! he would say. That was one answer he gave when he frequently heard the shocking declaration, "Why should I buy life insurance? When I die, that's their problem!" I used to wonder how anyone with a spouse and kids could say something like that; it simply blew me away.

My father had an even better response: "The Lord might provide, all right, but that provision might be a dingy tenement for your family to live in, and a washtub for your wife to sweat over. If you truly love your family, one of the cornerstones of life should be to pay an insurance company to take care of this responsibility for you."

My dad brought many new types of insurance to the island of Jamaica: casualty, health, and accident insurance (for cancer and other sicknesses as well as accidents), and manslaughter policies (since in that country, the car, not the driver, is insured, so every driver had to have insurance for both court costs and his defence). So when I emigrated to Canada in 1973, I was well prepared to make a career in the insurance business, since I believed profoundly in the concept.

I Turn Against My Beloved Profession

I soon had an excellent career, selling insurance and helping people to apply for life insurance, at Mutual Life of Canada, from 1974 to 1976. From the casualty insurance I had sold with my father back in Jamaica, I now entered the life insurance business, and I became a passionate promoter of the service.

But I also grew antagonistic and even hostile to insurance companies that sold RRSPs that were, in effect, registered whole life insurance policies — but the individual had zero cash value for seven years! And the salesman? He had the good fortune of being paid 130% of the premium/RSP contribution in the *first* year!

I soon realized that there is truly no such thing as life insurance. After all, we all will die, one day. Life insurance is simply something to fund that eventuality. Insurance companies will use mortality tables to figure out how long someone will "be here," they use interest rate assumptions to set up the sinking fund, and also purchase re-insurance to share the risk of what happens if you get knocked down while crossing the street.

But if you don't get hit by that truck, you'll be here a long time. And that ends up being a very long time to pay premiums into a sinking fund, where insurance companies for years have used an assumption of low interest rates — for example, 2% — while turning right around and actually loaning those premiums out at 8% in mortgages! Not a bad deal — for them. (In Toronto, one can see their tall, well-appointed, fully paid buildings up and down University Avenue.)

I slowly grew to recognize that insurance companies are phenomenally rich organizations precisely because they have consistently used the ignorance of most individuals to finance their coffers and make the people who own those companies very, very wealthy.

How wealthy? Well, the common stocks of insurance companies listed on the exchanges of the world are among the greatest businesses in the world; as I shall note several times in this book, the wildly successful Berkshire Hathaway holding company out of Omaha, Nebraska, is deeply engaged in the insurance business, because while those insurance firms are waiting those long years to pay the inevitable liability for one's injury or death, *they have the use of the money!* Several of the billions that Warren Buffett has so brilliantly invested in Coca-Cola, Gillette, and other internationally renowned businesses have come from the profits of the giant insurance companies that he owns. (Canadians are said to be "over-insured," but they are really over-*premiumed* and *under*-insured.)

What Drove Me Crazy about the Insurance Industry

One scenario really bothered me about the industry that I worked for with such passion and such determination, and it's a classic argument: Holders of life insurance can borrow against the "cash surrender value" of their policy, and use those proceeds as they wish.

Hardly. "Rip-off" is the best description I can use for this.

Let me explain. If you have, say, a $10,000 policy with $3,000 of cash value, you can borrow your own sinking fund (by this I mean the cash surrender value, which is the reserve, or sinking fund). So far, so good.

So, you borrow that money, while continually paying the premium on that $10,000 policy, along with the interest for that $3,000 loan. Fair enough. But then you drop dead, and what does the insurance company do? They will pay your beneficiaries only $7,000, because that $3,000 is considered an *advance* on the death benefit!

Things like that began to annoy me more and more. (I should mention that Canada has come a long way since I was in the insurance business over two decades ago, and it's only fair to note that the pushing of this type of insurance, certainly since the late 1980s, has subsided to a great degree.)

So, the insurance companies back then, and their many agents, would insist that whole life policies were the better deal. They weren't, of course. The bottom line is, people should insist that their insurance be pure insurance, by which I mean either term or straight insurance. There is simply no need whatsoever, in my opinion, for people to have any form of insurance with cash surrender value associated with it. Permanent or renewable term is *more* than sufficient, and a far better deal. (The idea, when I was in the industry, was that each person just had to have whole life, because you wanted to be able to convert it to term in your later years. But today there actually is permanent term, which goes straight up to the age of 100, so why blow all that money on the vastly more costly whole life, which comes with that utterly unnecessary "cash surrender value" built in?)

Naturally, some kind of life insurance is vitally important for estate planning purposes, and since I am always talking about creating "multi-generational wealth" with my clients, I cannot ignore the concept. The question is, what kind of life insurance will best allow their great-grandchildren to manage the wealth of *their* grandchildren, which I originally helped to create for them?

As I shall note frequently throughout this book, Revenue Canada is our partner. And on the death of the final spouse of a family, that institution deems that there is a disposition that took place to all the heirs. So, I believe it is essential to apply for life insurance on the joint lives of both husband and wife. This pays a tax-free lump sum on the last to die, whereas the premiums will stop at the death of the first spouse. Then, tax-free amounts of money are deposited to the estate, which creates liquidity. I suggest this on a continual basis, to avoid the destruction of a lifetime of estate and wealth building, and consider it an important part of estate and financial planning.

I Make the Leap from Insurance to Mutual Funds

What finally broke *this* camel's back was a classic ploy of the insurance industry two decades ago. They kept licensing an endless number of agents who kept bombing out of the business every month. So there was this continuous stream of new people coming in, putting new policies onto the books, and then soon leaving the business.

The insurance companies were constantly saying (if not in so many words), "Hey, all of you new agents! Give me the names of your friends and relatives, and I'll sell them insurance." But in order to leverage their constantly shifting human resources, they would be proclaiming this to many thousands of new agents. Of course, after each of those new agents left the insurance industry, they also left something else: their friends and relations to pay those (invariably too high) premiums indefinitely.

That is really what the insurance industry was all about, back then.

I remember going to see my closest friends and relatives,

to sell them insurance. One person I called upon was Phil Shearn. He and his wife, Rose, were friends from Jamaica, and I eagerly visited them with my branch manager at Mutual Life, Jack O'Neill, back in 1974.

We sold Phil a retirement savings plan; it was a Mutual Life of Canada policy called "R25 at 65." The plan meant that every $2,500 you deposited came due when you — the client — reached the age of 65. It was, quite literally, an endowment policy that would endow, at one's retirement age, exactly what the person put into it — with little or no interest whatsoever!

Not everyone lost from this deal, of course. It paid me over 100% of the first year's premium (!) or the RRSP contribution, over $4,000. I was thrilled.

But I really had no idea what I was doing for my clients — or to them. When Phil read the contract carefully, he quickly exercised his "recision rights," which essentially meant "I want my money back!"

When he explained to me what I had done to him, I was flooded with both shame and embarrassment. God knows, I was utterly mortified at my actions. It was a disgusting contract of insurance, sold under the guise of an RRSP.

I was mortified, all right — and furious. And so, I decided to launch a crusade against the insurance industry.

The first thing I did was to urge every client I had to purchase *only* (inexpensive and sufficient) term insurance, and to invest the cash surrender value into something worthwhile. (The rest of this book will be dedicated to showing you what is truly "worthwhile" investing in.)

I also helped to introduce new life insurance policies that carried a single premium that assumed a higher rate of interest. And so, I was soon visiting some of Hamilton, Ontario's most prominent businessmen and offering to replace their insurance — to double the face amount of the insurance for the cash surrender value in their current policies, and totally wipe out any future premiums.

Around this time, a friend of mine named James Bullock wrote a series of articles entitled "Life Insurance: The Myth and the Mystery" for the now-defunct business newspaper *The Financial Times of Canada*. His writings were so critical of that industry, I actually had fantasies that Jimmy and I might be assassinated by friends of the insurance companies because of our actions!

People like me were hardly alone in our "war" against the dubious workings of the insurance industry back in the 1970s, nor were these struggles limited to Canada alone. While I was personally replacing, on behalf of my clients, more whole life insurance policies with term insurance than you could imagine, there was a real uprising in the United States as well.

Indeed, a huge industry grew out of the then-dubious machinations of the insurance companies. The A. L. Williams group, which soon became one of the most successful groups in the United States and quickly came to Canada, is a case in point.

The story behind that company's origins was not dissimilar to the experiences of my friend Phil, who discovered how unfair his coverage was, and had raised my consciousness at the same time. The father of Mr. Williams was over-premiumed and under-insured, and when the man died prematurely his mother collected very little in way of benefits — after all those years of her husband paying huge sums of money. Unlike me, that family not only went to war against traditional insurance practices but actually created a mass movement across North America to "buy term and invest the difference."

Around this time, I met a remarkable individual and fellow Jamaican whom I consider one of my mentors and best friends to this day: Michael Lee-Chin. He was, and is, one of the most powerful people I've ever met, because of his amazing ability to implement what other people might consider "just a good idea."

I first met Mike in 1976 when he was working for Investors Group, one of Canada's major mutual funds companies. I had recently left Mutual Life of Canada and had formed an independent brokerage agency called Quantum. He had actually sought *me* out, and for a rather humorous reason: he had heard about "another very successful Jamaican fellow who also drives a Mercedes-Benz in Hamilton, Ontario"!

He wanted to recruit me to join him. He was unsuccessful at first, but we quickly formed an acquaintance and ultimately a friendship, as I spoke of my belief that most life insurance companies were exploiting people out of their ignorance. He, in turn, talked about the investment business through his then-still-captive-eyes of a representative at Investors — which sells only its own mutual funds.

By late 1978, Mike left Investors to open a branch office for Regal Capital Planners, and successfully recruited me to join him. And so, I finally became involved in the investment business. He would describe to me how well people who invested $10,000 in certain mutual funds did, compared with those who invested in various bank offerings, such as

Guaranteed Investment Certificates (or GICs), and I was overwhelmed! I was shaken by the concept of mutual funds and how they worked.

It would be fortunate that I had introduced Michael Lee-Chin to life insurance — the term kind, of course — because it would be life insurance sales that helped the two of us through the lean years of the 1981–84 recession, when high interest rates discouraged the purchase of mutual funds. During that rough time, we concentrated not only on selling term insurance, however, but also on estate planning.

Then, just before the stock market rebounded healthily in 1984, Michael came to me late one day at the office and exclaimed, "Richard, why not go and see your best insurance clients and tell them, 'If you don't believe that *now* is a fantastic time to invest, just give me $2,000 and I'll put it into four different mutual funds for you. We'll see what happens.' "

It was in this fashion that I built some of my most successful and faithful clients, who are with me to this day. In fact, there are several clients for whom I still keep that original $2,000 invested "on the books," just to remind them of the importance of being patient, long-term investors.

The importance of patience? More like the *genius* of patience. Each $500 I invested in mutuals such as Trimark Fund and Mackenzie Industrial American is now worth well over $5,000. What better proof could one have, for my proven, reliable, yet simple theory — which you shall read about throughout this book — of "buy quality investments and hold them long-term"?

And I Move On, in a Zig-Zag Course, to AIC Funds

Throughout the mid-1980s, Michael Lee-Chin and I sold mutual funds for Regal Capital Planners, which was then — and is still now — run by the admirable and wise Paul Rockel. He is a lovely man, and a true visionary in the mutual funds industry. He had a dramatic impact on me, as did Michael, as they each explained to me the value of mutual funds and professional management. I would not leave Regal until 1985.

Back then, I knew very little about the actual companies that handled and managed the mutual funds, nor was I at all aware of the concept of investing in publicly-traded securities on the stock markets of North America; I was simply a mutual funds salesman. I did a brief sojourn at Stuart Mutuals, and then finally, in the fall of 1987, joined my old friend Michael at Advantage Investment Counsel, alias AIC.

My first position was as branch manager of their Oakville office, and what I learned there is central to many of the themes and philosophies expressed throughout this book. AIC Funds had been a poorly performing group of mutual funds, which Michael Lee-Chin had purchased a few years earlier. And from 1985 to 1987, the managers of those so-so funds — which were nothing but a hodge-podge of equities — had no real focus or philosophy.

Then, the moment of truth: Michael decided to fire all those managers who had "come with the funds" he had purchased, and the two of us decided that we certainly could not do any worse than if we chose to implement the investment principles of Warren Buffett.

How right we were! It was at that moment, back in 1987,

when the AIC group of funds really started to take off, in both reputation and success.

I assisted Michael, as his senior vice-president of marketing, not only in building a sales force but in helping our salespeople to become passionately committed to our principles by a two-pronged approach: to build assets in mutual funds, and to help the Canadian public to invest, rather than speculate, in publicly-traded securities.

During those first, struggling years of the late 1980s, I would call on many brokerage firms and opened the door for future marketing opportunities for our own AIC marketing department, and I formed liaisons with major firms to promote our AIC funds. The ones responsible for their invariably wise and inspired purchases were Michael Lee-Chin, of course, and Jonathan Wellum. I knew every stock they chose, and had personal, in-depth knowledge of every business we invested in, because they were all discussed extensively with me. But I never picked any of them myself, as I never saw myself as a money manager. I am a theorist and a portfolio strategist, rather than a portfolio analyst.

Not that I *had* to pick them! Michael Lee-Chin was and is a brilliant strategist and implementer who would grab an idea and run with it; only then would he fine-tune it. "Ready, fire, AIM!" is the way he describes it. And in his hands, this kind of activity rarely failed. Highly motivated and caring, Michael, Jonathan, and I were all profoundly committed to the magnificent principles of Warren Buffett, which I shall discuss in depth in the pages to come.

In brief, we believed that stocks are parts of businesses, and not merely pieces of paper that one trades back and forth, like baseball cards. That's not a business or investing;

that's guesswork and gambling. Investors who sector rotate and asset allocate and market time are simply gamblers, not true investors. The only true investor is one who does what the variety-store-owner does: he buys a business, goes to work every day, and he earns money, slowly but surely. That's investing. And that's what was the difference between the philosophy of AIC Funds and every other mutual fund manager who calls himself a "money manager." (Since I am now instrumental in helping to develop a new family of mutual funds, Infinity, based on time-tested principles of a sound investment philosophy, I can now include myself in this same select group.)

Now, what do I mean by a sound investment philosophy? Read on!

2

A Recipe for Life
and Investing

WE all need role models in our lives. In many cases, it's our mother or our father; sometimes it's a world leader, such as a Gandhi or a Martin Luther King; other times, it's a poet, a scientist, a sports figure, even a movie star.

My recipe for success in life is quite straightforward:

- Identify a role model for yourself.
- Find his or her "recipe" for success.
- Implement it.

As you can see, there is no reinventing of the wheel going on here. Since I used the word "recipe," let me continue the metaphor. Imagine you are at a friend's home for dinner, and you are served a delicious bread pudding for dessert. You like it so much, you just have to have the recipe.

Provided you are given the exact measurements — the

correct amount of milk, bread, and raisins (and not "a pinch of this and a dash of that") — you could make the same bread pudding as your friend, because you had the recipe.

Well, imagine if you could get your hands on the recipe for successful investing. Before I give you the recipe, let me introduce you to the master chef — and certainly my own personal role model in my life as an investor — Warren Buffett. He is the richest and smartest businessman and investor in the United States, with a net worth in excess of $22 *billion* (and counting!) as of mid-1997.

In 1956, Mr. Buffett collected $105,100 from family and friends in Omaha, Nebraska, plus $100 from his own pocket, and started the Buffett Limited Partnership. This was an investment company in which he, as manager, received 25% of profit after investors received a 6% return on capital.

The fund prospered tremendously. Over its 13-year lifetime, the original investment compounded at 29.5% annually to reach about $100 million.

But by 1969, the market was so speculative and stock prices so high that Mr. Buffett could no longer find any companies that met his strict criteria for investing. So he folded the partnership, gave back most of the money to the shareholders, along with a proportional interest in a textile company called Berkshire Hathaway Inc., which he acquired in 1965.

The textile company, plagued by a history of financial troubles, finally closed. The new Berkshire Hathaway became a holding company, owning significant stakes in companies such as GEICO Corp., Gillette, Coca-Cola, Washington Post, Wells Fargo, General Dynamics Corp., and Salomon Brothers.

If you had put $10,000 in the original Buffett Limited Partnership, then converted to Berkshire Hathaway in 1965, your money would be worth over $200 million in 1997. This is, quite simply, the most successful investment of all time.

As you can see, Mr. Buffett is not only an investor but also a businessman, which brings me to the recipe. He believes in buying good businesses at good prices and staying with them as long as they remain good — and never selling, regardless of how high the stock price gets.

"What would be the point?" he asks. "You might invest the money in something *less* great!"

He does not try to time the stock markets or catch swings. "Don't try and figure out what the market is doing," he has said. "Figure out businesses you understand, and concentrate. Diversification is protection against ignorance, but if you don't feel ignorant, the need for it goes down drastically."

Mr. Buffett's Rip Van Winkle style of investing reflects his view that the stock market serves to move assets from the active to the patient. He says he knows of no individual or institution that has been successful at timing the market — "flitting from flower to flower," as he describes it. You will eventually sell your flowers to water your weeds.

Mr. Buffett does not buy stocks. Stocks are an abstraction. He buys *businesses*, or *parts of businesses* if the whole thing is not for sale. As he has said: "What I like is economic strength in an area I understand and where I think it will last. For example, it is very difficult to think of two companies in the world in important areas that have the presence of Coke and Gillette, two of Berkshire Hathaway's core holdings."

One of the most important times to reflect on the Buffett recipe and to be comforted by it is during severe stock market corrections or prolonged bear market periods. It is in those times that you will be forced to examine the inherent value in your stocks or mutual funds.

If your investment decisions were *not* based on a judgement about short-term prospects for the stock market, but rather reflected an opinion about long-term business prospects for specific companies, you would be less inclined to be upset and get scared out of your stocks at the wrong time.

Stock market corrections are a normal occurrence. They are not an abnormal phenomenon. Just like the changing seasons, if you know that corrections are inevitable, then you will be mentally prepared to be patient during them. You will hibernate with your stocks and mutual funds during the long winter, knowing that in the spring new growth will return.

As corporate earnings improve and stock markets head higher, articles of doom are appearing frequently in Canada and the United States, showing little sign of abating. The stock market is truly climbing a "wall of worry." These articles are a distracting annoyance because they are targeted at people's fear, which is destructive to their long-term investment objectives. It is interesting to note that as recently as 1990–91, *no* articles were forecasting the current buoyant markets. It seems some journalists take pleasure in trying to scare investors out of their mutual funds and stocks.

Several years ago, Mr. Buffett said in his annual report that if you're in a poker game and you don't know in the first half-hour who the patsy is, *you're* the patsy.

How does this apply to investing?

If the stock market goes down 10% and you want to buy more because the business is worth just as much, then the stock market is the patsy.

So, while anything can happen in stock markets, this does not have to concern the investor. The market crash of 1987 was probably an aberration caused by excessive computer program trading. Silly instruments cause silly prices. Astute investors can take advantage of these prices or ignore them.

The recipe for investing from the most successful investor of all time seems almost too simple. But then again, most things are.

What Is So Special about Mr. Buffett's Holding Company?

Berkshire Hathaway Inc. owns subsidiaries in a good number of diverse business activities. The most important of these is the property and casualty insurance business, conducted on both a direct and re-insurance basis through a number of subsidiaries, collectively referred to as the Berkshire Hathaway Insurance Group.

Investment portfolios of insurance subsidiaries include meaningful equity ownership percentages of other publicly-traded companies. At the end of 1996, these investments included 100% of the capital stock of GEICO Corporation — of which Berkshire Hathaway owned but 48% just three years earlier; approximately 13% of the capital stock of Capital Cities/ABC Inc., later exchanged for a healthy chunk of Walt Disney (3.6%); approximately 8.6% of The Gillette Company; approximately 8.1% of The Coca-Cola Company; approximately 15.8% of The Washington Post Company (which includes *Newsweek*); approximately 8% of the common stock of Wells Fargo & Company; approximately 10.5% of the common stock of General Dynamics Corporation, and common and convertible preferred stock of Salomon Inc., which have around 15% of the total voting power of that company.

If all that isn't diverse enough for you, Berkshire Hathaway Inc. also publishes the *Buffalo News*, a daily and Sunday newspaper in upstate New York. Other business activities conducted by non-insurance subsidiaries include publication and distribution of encyclopedias and related educational and instructional material (World Book and Childcraft products), manufacture and marketing of home cleaning systems and related accessories (sold principally under the Kirby name), manufacture and sale of boxed chocolates and other confectionery products (See's Candies), retailing of home furnishings (Nebraska Furniture Mart), manufacture and distribution of uniforms (Fechheimer Brothers Company), manufacture, import, and distribution of footwear (H. H. Brown Shoe Company, Lowell Shoe, Inc., and Dexter Shoe Company), and manufacture and distribution of air compressors, air tools, and painting systems (Campbell Hausfeld products).

There are several other businesses owned by Mr. Buffett's Berkshire Hathaway, each engaged in a variety of other — invariably successful — activities. All of them are seemingly "ordinary" businesses, which produce extraordinary returns.

Once again, Warren Buffett's track record has been nothing less than phenomenal. It is interesting and informative that Berkshire Hathaway is the single most highly priced security listed on any exchange in any country in the world. In late 1996, when I first wrote these words, a single share on the New York Stock Exchange was worth over $33,000; in late June 1997, it had reached $47,700! Yet only four years ago, one could snap up that same share for little over $20,000. And just a few years before that, around $6,000.

Not bad.

If you were not familiar before now with either Mr. Buffett or his astonishing holding company, Berkshire Hathaway, you may have been taken aback a little by the variety of the businesses: car insurance? soft drinks? razor blades? newspapers? home cleaning systems? encyclopedias? chocolates? shoes? furniture? What on earth could they all have in common?

(Do you recall the excellent point made in that best-selling business book of the 1980s, *In Search of Excellence*? "Stick to the Knitting!" the authors warned all potential business-people. If you are in computers, don't sell detergents on the side! And look what happened when Gerber's, the baby food people, started to expand into other, unrelated fields? They lost millions upon millions of dollars!)

But there is something critically and profoundly similar about all the businesses owned (or partly owned) by Mr. Buffett's company: they are all — every single one of them — superior businesses with strong economic fundamentals, which were purchased at good, fair prices, and which have never been sold, as long as they remain good businesses.

Remember what I said earlier in this chapter: to Warren Buffett — and to me, since he is my mentor — the stock market is utterly and totally irrelevant. (I'll have more to say about this later.) The only purpose it really serves is as a reference, to see who is offering to do something stupid — sell us shares of a good business at a very low price.

Far too many of us — probably the vast majority of us — need immediate gratification from the stock market's daily listings ("Look! ABC Inc. went up 2 points!" "Oh, no! My shares of XYZ Ltd. have fallen one-quarter! What am I to do?") in order to validate our well-being, our sense of emotional, if not financial, self-worth.

The only thing that matters to Warren Buffett — and to me — is the quality of the businesses he owns. Mr. Buffett sees the stock market, in the short term, as a voting machine that requires a voter registration test based only on money, and not on emotional stability or on intelligence. In the long run, it is a weighing machine. But if the quality of the businesses one buys is good, with strong earnings, then eventually one will have higher stock prices. (And note that I write "eventually"; those higher stock prices do not necessarily come overnight, or in the next few weeks.)

What has that philosophy done for Mr. Warren Buffett of Omaha, Nebraska? It has given him a net worth of over $22 billion in mid-1997. (That net worth was only around $9.5 billion three years ago.)

"Ahh," you may say, "this Buffett guy is pretty impressive, but what about *risk*? I'm terrified to risk my money — and the money that my spouse, my children, and I will need in the future — on something as insecure as the stock market or mutual funds. What should I do?"

Several things. Such as reading the next chapter.

3

Let's Define "Risk"

I believe that we are on the verge of an epidemic crisis of monolithic proportions. A huge army of men and women, known as Baby Boomers — defined roughly as those born between 1946 and 1964 and numbering close to 80 million in the United States alone — will be marching into and through middle age and old age over the next three or four decades. (The latest demographics tell us that, every eight minutes, another person turns 50!) The vast majority of those people will be unprepared and under-capitalized, because they did not understand "risk," or how inflation will erode the purchasing ability of their capital.

We must, therefore, learn to properly define risk. I define that word in two ways, quantitatively and qualitatively. In other words, how much risk is there, and what is the quality of that risk?

A good example: A woman invests in a powerful business

like Atlanta-based Coca-Cola; a man chooses to drive to Niagara Falls, Ontario, for the weekend, and play the roulette wheel or try his skill at the blackjack table at their new casino.

Both are taking risks. But surely we can determine that even though both activities *involve* risk, the quality and the quantity of each are vastly different.

The real problem with how most of us view risk is that the majority of us learned our definition of risk (and safety) from our parents, who in turn learned it from their parents. And the latter were, by and large, children of the Great Depression — those long, hungry, insecure, and terrifying years of the 1930s.

Peter Lynch, in his bestseller *Beating the Street*, notes that the stock market crash of 1929 and the Great Depression that followed are both responsible for having kept two generations of potential investors away from share ownership, yet it has been inflation and taxes that have done more damage to erode capital than a *dozen* stock market crashes could ever have accomplished!

In 1893, just three generations ago, the life expectancy of the average individual in North America was a mere 33 years; just one century later, that expectancy is well over 70 for men, close to 80 for women. This has led to great changes in our attitudes towards our health. Today, a person dreading the winter and entering the flu season might say to himself, "I'd better not catch the flu; I might have to take a week off work." Yet only a single generation ago, he may have declared, "I hope I don't get the flu, because I might die."

In these last few years of the twentieth century, a man or woman who makes it to 60 stands a good chance of living well into his or her nineties. The man will live a decade or two longer than his father, while his wife could well live a full decade longer than her now-long-lasting spouse!

In my opinion, the traditional financial services industry has (tragically) done a good job of discrediting patient, long-term investing in the shares of great businesses — the Warren Buffett way — and instead promises results from speculative and aggressive trading practices that generate commissions on every transaction. The only people who made money from these all-too-common actions were the *brokers*, not the clients. It was as if pharmacists kept pushing you to purchase drugs you didn't need (thus earning fees from each prescription), or doctors who run medical labs insisted on frequent but unnecessary tests that were a total waste of time for all involved but drummed up great business for their technicians.

Nothing on the face of this earth can provide you with the capital appreciation that owning shares of the world's great businesses will give you. Furthermore, by owning those shares of quality companies, history has shown that you never have to take spectacular actions (or even the slightest risks) to achieve spectacular results.

A single, quite striking example: There has never been a time in the past eight decades that you, your parents, or your grandparents should not have been permanent share-holders of Coca-Cola.

In 1919, Coke went public at $40 a share. In 1993, those shares, held for nearly 70 years with all dividends reinvested, were worth over $2.2 million each! (As of mid-1997, that number was actually over $5.5 million — more than double again, in less than four years.) But let's not go back that far. In 1938, when most of our parents had at least a few dollars to risk, a fresh $40 then invested in Coca-Cola would be worth $25,000 by the end of 1993, and many thousands more, by mid-1997. Between 1983 and 1993, Coca-Cola ranked number 72 out of the top 100 performing businesses listed on the New York Stock Exchange, with a return of over 1,200%. In fact, $100,000 invested in 1983 was worth over $1.2 million only a decade later, and more than double that amount by the summer of 1997.

Even shorter term: When Warren Buffett of Berkshire Hathaway chose to invest a *further* $1.23 billion into Coca-Cola in the spring of 1989, the value of these shares of Coke had increased to nearly $5 billion five years later, and well over $10 billion today! This is what happens when a company — a great, powerful company like Coca-Cola — produces an annualized total return (stock appreciation plus dividends) of approximately 28%, between 1981 and the middle of 1996.

What Battle Are We Fighting Here?

Some believe that the battle is knowledge versus ignorance. In many cases, it is. But as in the case of so much of investing, the real battle is fear versus faith.

Twenty years ago, if someone sat in their broker's office and exclaimed, "No, I do *not* want to own a portfolio of the world's greatest businesses," he was termed "a risk-averse investor."

This is an oxymoron, like "live recording" or "military intelligence." That foolish individual was *not* an investor, nor was he "risk averse." He was a saver.

Most of us have been taught, whether by teachers or by parents — all of whom suffered through the Great Depression either directly or through their respective families' horror stories of riding the rails, selling apples on street corners, or ubiquitous soup kitchens — that saving is a wise and intelligent thing to do.

I disagree. A saver is someone who looks back into the past with fear. He does not want to own anything, and only hopes to lend his money short-term, and for a guarantee (read Guaranteed Investment Certificate; read Canada Savings Bond), because he is *always* expecting the next Armageddon, the next crash, the next depression.

That's not the way the wise investor acts. He or she looks forward into the future with faith, and believes in the possibilities and recognizes the benefits of owning businesses — or shares of them, which can be just as worthwhile.

Indeed, our poor investor was not really "risk averse" — he was "loss averse." He did not understand the essential difference between temporary fluctuations in the value of shares of great businesses and the loss of principal.

What it all comes down to is this: Canadians and Americans are notoriously bad investors who are self-destructive when managing their personal portfolios. They get most of their information from the news media (which I like to call the Antichrist of investing), while neglecting advice from dedicated professionals.

What they do instead is pathetic: They rely upon the no-load (or the "no-help," as I like to call it) mutual fund industry. These bad-advice people, as I like to call them, also include the banks, which are recent players in the world of mutual funds. So, when "GIC refugees" asked their bank teller, in 1994, to put them into "that fund that pays 40% a year," they were sold bond funds that promptly declined in value as interest rates rose. It was a case of inexperienced people advising inexperienced people who did not wish to invest in mutual funds in the first place!

Is there a risk in the world of equities? I believe that the greatest risk — the most dangerous risk, indeed, the mother of all risks — in equities is in *not owning them at all*. And people who allow themselves to be distracted by the current apocalypse du jour will live to regret it. What's interesting about the current apocalypse du jour is that it's much like the cross-town bus: if you miss one of them, you can be sure that another will come along in a few minutes.

The real risk in not investing is not the risk of principal loss. No, that's simply a minor risk. The real risk of not investing is the continuous erosion of your capital while you are alive.

The best example of this tragic condition is only a few feet away from where you are now sitting, at least if you are like me. Look into your pantry, and note the price of the can of beans way in the back: 29 cents? 39 cents? And the price of the can that you recently bought "on sale" — 79 cents.

Or look through some of the old letters you have saved from loved ones, mailed to you years ago. That 10-cent U.S. stamp would get a letter across the breadth of the United States in 1974. Ten years later, it would take a 20-cent U.S. stamp to get the same service. Today, the cost has more than tripled, to 32 cents, to mail a letter across the United States.

In Canada, in 1974, a stamp cost 8 cents. Just over twenty years later, the cost is nearly 50 cents, when one includes the GST. Over *six times the cost*, in less than a quarter-century, to mail the same letter in Canada! These are but a few common, yet quite dramatic, examples of inflation in North America.

(We often pride ourselves on how low the inflation rate is in Canada and the United States, and with good reason; the horrors of runaway inflation that have been seen in Germany, Argentina, Russia, and many Middle Eastern countries since the 1920s have often been nightmarish, with clerks changing prices hourly on articles of clothing and produce. Still, those dust-covered cans of beans in the back of our pantry, and those envelopes lovingly saved in our closets with those "cheap" stamps on their upper-right-hand corners, should give us pause, even in this country, and even over the past few decades.)

It is vital that we learn to ignore the worries of the world long enough to allow our investments in the great businesses of our times to be successful. On July 8, 1932, the Dow Jones industrials recorded an intra-day low of 40.56. On January 31, 1994, the same Dow Jones recorded an intra-day high of 4,000. (Need I even mention the level of 6,000, reached in the early fall of 1996, barely two and a half years later? Or 6,500, just a few short weeks after that, and 7,000, in early 1997?) And over 7,600 in the summer of 1997? Over those six-plus decades, more wealth was created for the share-holders of North American businesses than at any other period in the history of the world, and more than any other asset class in existence.

The key to success in investing is to *ignore* the market, and its so-called risks, and patiently hold strong "earning machines" known as businesses — and for the long haul.

As of 1997, as I write these words, inflation is lower than it has been in years, but it is always present, always ready to eat up savings and increase prices. There is a dragon in all of our lives, and it consists of inflation and rising costs, pushing us towards the agonizing dilemma of outliving our capital. But there is a St. George, too, to help slay that killer dragon: the ownership of great businesses, like the ones that Warren Buffett has purchased for his Berkshire Hathaway holding company; businesses that are always finding new and exciting ways of making money for their shareholders.

Less than a decade ago, we all experienced — through radio, TV, and newspapers — the most significant world event since Christopher Columbus happened upon the New World: the fall of communism and the tearing down of the Berlin Wall.

This was not only a political victory, of course. It was an economic victory for The People, who are the true, practising capitalists of the world. In the first hours after the wall was torn down, millions of men and women crossed over into freedom, just to see what it felt like to walk into West Germany without being shot. Three questions were heard, over and over again, as the most asked that fateful night. They were:

"Where is McDonald's?"

"Where can I buy Levi's?"

"Where can I buy a Coke?"

Echoing these extraordinary phrases, in terms of the stunningly powerful impact of great companies with universally recognized brand names, is a line recently expressed by Warren Buffett: "It is very comforting to go to bed at night knowing that over 2.5 billion males will get up in the morning and shave with Gillette."

As I noted at the start of this chapter, we are on the cusp of a global capitalist revolution. Never before in history have the world's great businesses been given true access to over

6 billion people around the globe — many of whom would love to have their own phone, their own car, or simply to purchase a hamburger and a glass of Coke, while sitting in their Levi's jeans.

And to think that many people wonder why Warren Buffett has put such faith in such "simple" things as soft drinks, razor blades, newspapers, shoes, and furniture!

It's because he doesn't believe in risk. Or in fear. Or in "saving."

Only through true investing — *intelligent, long-term investing in quality businesses* — will our futures be assured, and the inevitable risks of inflation and rising costs be vanquished.

4

Five Key Steps to
Creating Your Fortune

I N the last chapter, I only hinted at the quite frightening picture that will speak to a large percentage of North Americans when they turn 65 or 70: the prospect of poverty, of despair, of diminishing lifestyle, even of hunger. (Or maybe you expect the federal and provincial governments to actually continue the pensions and social insurance that we've counted on for so many decades? And even if they do, do you honestly believe it will be enough for you and your spouse to live on?)

In early November 1996, my worst fear came walking into my office. Mr. and Mrs. Johnson (I'll call them), aged 86 and 80. They were brought to me by a friend, who somehow expected me to work a miracle for them.

And a miracle was what they needed. This couple had been retired for 26 years, and had just about exhausted the principal of their savings, *because they had never invested.*

"Why on earth didn't the two of you invest?" I asked them.

"Because we were afraid of losing our money," was their reply.

In other words, they did not invest because they feared poverty. But by not investing, they had brought about the very thing that they had most feared! These two elderly people had come to my office with only $35,000 to their names, and expected me to turn it into an adequate income investment to support them for the rest of their lives! I didn't like their chances, but I tried my best for them.

The Johnsons should have been investing over the course of their long lives, but instead, they made a commitment to buy those always-safe, always-reliable (and always-disappointing) GICs, which let them down terribly. This would be a good place to quote from a powerful letter to the editor of the *Globe and Mail*'s Report on Business section, published on October 21, 1996. Sadly, it came out too late to help that pathetic elderly couple in my office, who came to me only a few weeks later. Written by Tom Connolly of Cobourg, Ontario, it was responding to an earlier letter that had expressed "shock" that three York University professors had suggested that "retirees would be better off with more equities." I quote from the letter:

> To fund retirement, one should consider dividend income, not gains from trading. A retiree should buy and hold good-quality common stocks.
>
> For instance, if an investor had purchased Bank of Nova Scotia common stock in the fall of 1990 when it was trading at $11.12, the investor would now be receiving a dividend of $1.36 a share or 12% on the investment.

After factoring in the benefit of the Canadian dividend tax credit, the yield is in the order of 16%. I can easily fund my retirement lifestyle with a yield of 16%. Furthermore, this 16% does not include gains on the stock price, and next year the dividend will go up again.

Alternatively, in the fall of 1990, an investor could have opted for a five-year guaranteed investment certificate paying 11.25%. Last fall, the GIC would have had to be renewed at 6.5% — a decrease in income of 42.7%. [Author's note: By the fall of 1996, you could not get a GIC paying more than $2\frac{1}{2}$% — for a stunning *decrease* of income of *well over 80%*.]

Common stocks can provide an increasing income so that retirees do not have to spend capital. The income from a bond is fixed and cheapens with inflation.

It was all so sad. Nothing this couple could have done, other than gambling their money away at a casino, could have given them as disappointing a result as what they were getting from their GICs. The worst mutual fund in the world would not have treated them more horribly, and Mr. and Mrs. Johnson were in dire straits.

They had played into their own fears, which told them that to buy shares in a bank might be dangerous, but to buy GICs or Canada Savings Bonds, and live on the interest, would be safe. And so they sat in my office, with $35,000 to their names.

What could I do for a couple in the twilight of their years on this earth? I explained to them that there was always a possibility that we could have a stock market correction, and that they should not panic if there was one. I told them that I could not practise any kind of "market timing," because I didn't believe in that, and had no idea if or when it would go down. And then I suggested that they invest in a quality mutual fund that handled a portfolio of superior businesses, such as bank stocks, Bombardier, Canwest Global, Trimark, Coca-Cola, AmEx, Berkshire Hathaway, and others of that quality.

I have been thinking of that couple as I work on this chapter, because they fit so perfectly — and so pathetically — into a theory that I have long held about investing: Every reader of this book must imagine that *you, today,* are confronting *your own self,* when you will be in your late middle age.

So there you are — 25, 35, 50, or whatever your age is at the moment you are reading this — meeting your own self, when you will be 45, 35, or 20 years older.

I don't know how to make this any less painful, so I'll scream it out in capital letters and bold it, to boot: YOU ARE THE CUSTODIAN OF THAT OLDER MAN OR WOMAN!

I'm sure you'd agree that you are responsible for that older person within you. And if each of us is, indeed, the custodian of the older man or woman we will someday become, then you'd better have some pretty good answers to his or her awkward, and possibly mortifying, questions.

Here are some possibilities of what might transpire for many of us:

Your older self: It's good to meet you.

You, today: Uh, well, it's good to meet you, too!

Your older self: Thanks for giving up smoking.

You, today: It was easy, really. I'm just sorry I didn't do it a lot earlier.

Your older self: Okay, let's get down to business. So, how much money have you put away for me?

You, today: Geez. Look, I . . .

Your older self: I mean, what's my net worth now? You've had several decades to invest, you know. Did you prepare for my — hell, for *our* — future? Where's the nest egg? Will I be able to live in the way that I was accustomed to, as the divorce lawyers like to insist on behalf of their clients? Where are the investments?

You, today: Listen, please! Do you know the cost of a house in a Canadian city nowadays? What it cost to feed and clothe those kids? And now that they are heading off to university . . .

Your older self: I'm devastated. I'm sick at heart. Did you never think of me when you were starting out? Didn't you know that I was *inside* of you? What could you have been thinking? *Or were you even thinking at all?*

The point of my playlet is abundantly clear: the vast majority of everything you earn does, of course, belong to you, but you are the custodian of the 65- or 70-year-old person within you (and whom you will eventually become), and if you do not put aside at least 10% of your income for this individual, you have robbed him or her. You have spent that older person's money — and no excuses will be sufficient. I think again of that sad couple in their 80s, sitting in my office that day.

There's a witty bumper-sticker that I've seen on dozens of cars over the past decade, which reads: "We Are Busy Spending Our Children's Inheritance." Well, it may be witty when it comes to your children (although I personally doubt that, if you think deeply about it; don't we all wish to leave our children something, to make their lives easier than we had it?). But when the bumper-sticker is applied to your older self, it becomes bitter, ugly, even heart-breaking.

Since this can get pretty depressing, I'd better turn to some advice, and quickly. (After all, that older self in every one of you readers is getting closer to reality every second, right?) There will be tons of advice in this book, but here is the perfect place to give you several Real Winners — and ones that, if followed thoughtfully, will inevitably make you a winner as well.

Speaking of winners, I am suddenly reminded of a brilliant comment by Warren Buffett, my hero and mentor, who is quoted frequently in this book: "People would rather be offered a winning lottery ticket than a chance to get rich slowly."

I agree with him. And I join him in his belief that this truism is a very, very sad comment about human nature. A pretty self-destructive one, too. Okay, here goes . . .

5

First Law:
Pay Yourself First

THIS First Law of Creating Wealth might seem a bit obvious, but like most deep thoughts, there is a lot going on
here. Recall what I've been saying about how every one of us
is the custodian of an older gentleman or gentlewoman of the
same name who is in his or her later years of life. You haven't
met that person yet, but I can assure you, the vast majority
of us will feel pretty terrible when we are told that we've not
done a good job with that person's net worth, because, as
noted, we are the custodian of that man or woman.

If we lived above our means, or spent more than we
earned, or did not set aside at least a portion of our income,
then we have been robbing that older person who dwells in
every one of us.

In other words, we must make sure that we are *not* a
poor custodian of that elderly soul who will someday walk in
our shoes.

This is what I mean by pay yourself first. This means nothing more or less than setting aside (and investing wisely; more on that later) one-tenth to one-fifth of everything you earn for your retirement — and from your earliest years possible.

Many years ago, I came across a story called "The Richest Man in Babylon," and although I haven't seen it for ages it made a real impact on me and my thinking. Just the other day, I was told that a portion of this story has been reprinted in textbooks that every financial planner has to study in order to earn a licence. See if it does the same for you, in my retelling.

Babylon was, of course, an advanced society that existed on this earth several thousand years before Christ. It had magnificent buildings, grand monuments, complex institutions, and was, inarguably, one of the most sophisticated civilizations that ever existed.

Not unlike us today, they stored their information on hard disks — but in their case, it was words baked onto clay tablets. Fortunately, several of these have been discovered in the sand, which is, apparently, the perfect preserver for these documents.

Several hunks of clay told the story about the richest man in the great city of Babylon, whose name was Arkad, who, apparently, was the first financial planner in history. The conversation he had with a young man, if my memory serves me correctly, went something like this:

Young man: How did you come to be the richest man in all of Babylon?

Richest man: Before I answer your question, I have a few questions for you.

Young man: Very well, sir.

Richest man: Do you earn a living?

Young man: I have a job and a salary, yes.

Richest man: What do you do with that money?

Young man: Like everyone else, I suppose, I pay the rent on my home, I buy bread, shoes, clothes . . .

Richest man: It seems to me that you are doing an excellent job of spending your income on the goods and services that are provided by all of those people in our community. Indeed, you are helping to make them all wealthy, since they are all in business to make money, right?

Young man: I suppose so . . .

Richest man: But what are you doing for yourself?

Young man: What on earth do you mean, sir?

Richest man: Quite simple, really: What are you paying yourself?

Young man: Why, nothing, of course! I'm busy paying everyone else!

I don't recall if there was anything else on that tablet, but there is really nothing more needed to make the point. That man did not become the richest man in Babylon by accident, I can assure you! Here is, arguably, the earliest document in history of prudent, thoughtful financial planning. And this "law," if you wish, remains fundamental to *all* investing to this very day, several thousand years after it was (quite literally) set in stone: pay yourself first. Otherwise, you will pay everyone else first — whether it be for light bills, heating, car payments, gas, whatever — and end up making everyone else in the world wealthy, and never doing the same thing for yourself.

This leads me to two of those questions that we often ask ourselves when we are very young — "Why am I here on this earth?" "Why do I exist?" — but then we get so caught up in pubescence, school, university, love, marriage, having children, working, and a thousand other things that we rarely confront them again.

The Big Questions we must ask here are, Why do we work? and, not unrelated, Why do businesses exist?

Think about the latter for a moment: Why *is* your (friendly neighbourhood) bank — whether the Royal, the Bank of Montreal, Chase Manhattan, whomever you choose to deal with — in business? Why is Esso or Petrocan in business? Why is General Motors, Ford, Chrysler, or Honda in business?

The answer is incredibly simple. It's for one reason only: to create wealth for their shareholders, and maximize that wealth.

The next Big Question soon follows: How do they create that wealth for their shareholders? The answer to this query is a bit more complicated, and depends upon the kind of business. In the case of the banks, by taking your savings and lending it to other people who will pay good interest for it — which in turn creates wealth for their shareholders. As for the oil companies and the auto makers, it is by buying petroleum at one price and selling it at a higher price, and by convincing you that your miserable car is outdated and you really need a new one.

This may seem extremely obvious to the casual reader, but I see it as one of the great secrets I discovered in my decades of work in the investment field: Why (do these businesses exist)? And how (do they make their shareholders wealthy)?

In life, these questions demand far more complex answers:

We exist to love, to create families, to help our communities, to spiritually connect with others and with our Creator to try to have an effect on our loved ones, and sometimes even on our society and world. But in the world of business, it's far more clear-cut: Businesses are in business to make money for the people who own them (whether their president, their employees, their shareholders — anyone with a stake in their success and survival).

There is something sad in the lives of the billions of people who do not have a financial interest in one or more businesses, and it can be described in a rather pathetic, Sisyphean manner. (You remember the tragic Greek character Sisyphus, don't you? The gods condemned him to roll a giant rock up the side of a mountain for eternity. When the rock nearly reached the top, it would always roll back down — forcing poor Sisyphus to start all over again.)

If you'd like to see a modern example of Mr. Sisyphus, simply look around you: The vast majority of people are very much like the young questioner of "The Richest Man in Babylon," are they not? They work, out of the need to purchase bread so they can sustain themselves to go and work, to buy bread to sustain themselves, to go to work, to buy bread to sustain themselves, to go to work . . . You get the idea.

This was an awful experience for the ancient Greek Sisyphus, and it is, alas, a similarly awful experience for the vast majority of humanity. (The great French existentialist philosopher Albert Camus once wrote an essay about that tragic hero, concluding that he must "make believe he is happy." But I believe that most of us would prefer a more attractive kind of existence during our brief stay on this earth.)

This is where the First Law of Wealth — that you must pay yourself first — comes in. Because only by paying ourselves first — and through wise financial planning that flows directly from this single fact — can we avoid the Sisyphean existence described above.

Yes, only through paying ourselves first, setting aside a regular chunk of money — no matter how small that chunk is — will that magical component of Compound Interest Over Time take care of the size of that investment. Only in this way can one break the deadly cycle of work–bread–work–bread–work. And when this cycle of working-just-to-sustain-ourselves is shattered, one may replace it with one, legitimate, crucial goal that we all have, but too rarely achieve: financial freedom. That is what paying yourself first is really all about.

Okay, now. Another quick quiz: What are the three things that any person can do with his or her money?

I'm being rhetorical here; here's the easy answer: The only three things that one can do with money are:

- lend it,
- spend it, or
- invest it.

You have probably guessed by now which one I propose for every reader of this book, if you wish to avoid pushing giant financial boulders up giant mountains for the rest of your life. (And you already know what happens when the rock reaches the top. It's a tough world out there.)

To be blunt, the choice is yours, no matter how strapped you find yourself at this moment, what with rent or mortgage, kids' clothes or schoolbooks, job security or even job search. Let's look at each possibility.

If you lend it, you do not get invited to any bondholders' meetings. There is simply no such thing. Only shareholders get those fancy meetings, where they get to eat caviar and enjoy the benefits of being a stakeholder among other shareholders in this or that business.

Bondholders — who have (foolishly) chosen to lend their money to a bank or a government — are paid only a medium rate of interest. (As the great American TV comic Ernie Kovacs once noted, "They call television a 'medium' because it's not rare, and it's not well done." The same can be said about the rate of interest of bonds.)

Let's be honest here: The day that you can lend your money to a government or an institution and make a better return than you could by investing that same money in the stock of that institution is the day that that business would stop being in business. To put this another way, if you chose to lend your money to, say, the Royal Bank, and you actually earned more money than you did from investing in the Royal's stock, the bank would have no reason to exist! Please remember my thought, stated above, about why any business is in business: to generate profits and to create wealth for its shareholders. And the way banks accomplish this is, of course, by taking someone's savings (or lending of money, if you wish), and lending it to others at a profit!

When Polonius lectures his son Laertes in Shakespeare's *Hamlet* and pompously declares, "Neither a borrower nor a lender be," he knew what he was talking about, even if much of his other advice was pretty stupid. Lending is a fool's game — even though every bank, trust company, and insurance agency spends millions on advertising to try to talk you into doing it. Ignore all their pleas; they are only doing what businesses *have* to do to stay in business: make money.

Please, let them make their money from someone else if you don't wish to betray the 65- or 70-year-old person whom you shall become in the near (or distant) future. You are their custodian, remember?

So much for the first thing a person can do with money — lend it. I say, *don't do it.* The banks can manage just fine without you, I promise.

The second thing one can do with one's money, spend it, is self-evident. We all must spend, and, living in a consumer-driven society, we are all constantly reminded — by tens of thousands of commercials every single day, from TV to radio to giant billboards to the ubiquitous sides of buses and sub-ways — about how it is our moral obligation to spend. (As the old joke goes, "Money can't buy you happiness; it can only buy you the things that can *make* you happy.") We are forced to spend on goods and services from companies who are in the business to make money for their shareholders.

I am not about to tell anyone not to spend their money, especially after they've shelled out nearly twenty bucks for this book. And I sense that most readers would agree that it's a lot more fun to live in a nice apartment or house than it is to survive inside an old refrigerator carton on a cold city street. So go and spend. But don't spend everything — which leads me to the third thing we can do with money: invest it.

When one invests, especially in quality businesses, whether through common stocks or trustworthy mutual funds, one is actually purchasing a chunk — no matter how tiny — in those businesses, which is precisely how businesses grow, and how we *all* grow wealthier and better able to care for that older man or woman whom we shall inevitably become.

And the best single way to invest is — you guessed — *to pay yourself first*.

Which leads us to the Second Law of Wealth Creation.

6

Second Law: Set Goals

GOALS are nice things to have, as Wayne Gretzky will be happy to tell you; he makes $5 million U.S. a year (and more than that when you include the many endorsements) scoring them. But most of you are aware that the famous hockey player had a father who would sprinkle water on his backyard every winter, put his then-toddler-aged son into tiny skates, and make him go through hours of practice, to teach him how to reach (well, to score) those well-paying goals.

The same goes for financial goals, of course. Nebulous goals such as "I wanna be rich!" are not what I'm talking about here. I'm suggesting that we should all set goals that will define what our wealth is, and will be in the future.

Assuming that you are reading this book in the comfort of your home in the evening — and there is nothing good on TV anyway — let me talk about how you got to work this morning. You may think of it as a simple goal, but you still had to go through quite a bit of planning in order to achieve it:

- You knew that you had to be at the office by, say, 8:45 a.m.
- You decided how you would get there: car, train, bus, bicycle, roller-blading, jogging, whatever.
- You decided on the time you had to leave your home in order to get to work.
- You chose what route you would take.
- You had already figured out the amount of time you needed to brush your teeth, shower, shave, get dressed, and grab some kind of breakfast, and possibly even put together a lunch as well.

Not bad! You really do know how to set goals, don't you?

You can already see what I'm getting at here, and the images I have used are clearly related to Rule Number Two: In thoughtful financial planning, it is essential, when you set your goals about your present and future money needs, to know which route to take, and what vehicle you should use, to help you arrive at your proper financial destination. (And when — having to be at work by 8:45 a.m. is a lot less complex than your ultimate goal of achieving money stability at 60, 65, 70, or whenever.)

The term "vehicle" is a nice pun here, since it works well. For instead of "car" or "subway," I'm referring to such "financial vehicles" as mutual funds, publicly-traded securities, limited partnerships, and so on; any or all could play a role in getting you to your final financial destination at the proper time.

Let me be a bit dramatic here; please bear with me: I would rather stick needles in my eyes than lend *any* of my money to a government (read Canada or U.S. Savings Bonds) or an institution (read bank or trust company) by buying a bond or a term deposit. (At least when you stuff money into your mattress, you may be able to get a good night's sleep from the additional softness.) And, as you may have suspected, I am against anyone, especially myself, sticking needles into their eyes. Almost as heartily as I frown upon foolish money-wasting "loans" of any kind.

You already know what I do favour and what I urge — no, beg — every reader to move towards in their life: achieve business ownership through purchase of quality equities (i.e., stocks).

Let's play with this goal-setting concept for a while, shall we?

I could give hundreds of pages of examples, but let's just try one or two. There is a gentleman who is 50 years old this year, and he hopes to retire in 15 years, with an annual income of $50,000 a year.

Problem: If there is an inflation of 5% a year — please recall when it hit over 12% annually, back in the late 1970s, so that's not an outrageous assumption, in spite of the low inflation rate in 1997, as I write these words — this individual will actually need $104,000 a year in 15 years in order to purchase the same goods and services that his dreamed-of $50,000 a year was buying him a decade and a half earlier.

This means that the gentleman must have a nest egg of over $1 million in order to take out that $104,000.

The question is, Who of us knows what we have to accomplish in order to achieve the financial goal of having $1 million stashed away 15 years from today?

The answer? Very, very few of us. Using traditional vehicles (and I don't mean Honda or Mercedes here), one would have to set aside in excess of $42,000 after tax, at 7% after tax, and you've got your million bucks. The problem is, these numbers double to $84,000 before tax and where on earth can you find a lender who will pay 14% so that you can net 7% after tax?

I could give countless other examples, but I sense that this one is sufficient.

There is a good expression that captures the Second Rule of Wealth extremely well: "If you fail to plan, you plan to fail."

How true.

7

Third Law:
Be a Contrarian

WE always complain when our children are "contrary," but I urge everyone to go the "contrarian" route, when it comes to investing and amassing wealth.

Remember poet Robert Frost's famous line about "taking the road less travelled"? (It "made all the difference," he notes at the end of that poem.) Think about driving along a congested highway — a thought that won't be much of a stretch for readers who live in any of Canada's metropolitan areas. You listen to the traffic reports over the radio, which warn you of overturned tractor-trailers, crowded roads, and endless traffic jams.

So you (finally) decide to beat the traffic by pulling off the highway and quite literally — if not literarily — taking the road less travelled. You now drive along side roads or streets that are not clogged with other people's cars. And you realize at once that you are moving faster than ever because there's hardly anyone else on that road. Pretty smart, eh?

The above paragraphs are, I feel, an excellent metaphor for the contrarian way of investing: If you take that less-travelled road in investing, you'll be a lot better off — and you'll reach your ultimate destination (in the financial case, money-freedom, or a more lucrative retirement) much, much quicker.

I am convinced of this. If you do what everybody else does — whether driving on a major thoroughfare, or investing in the same manner as most others — you will end up like everybody else. And that just isn't good enough.

Think of the major societies of the world over the past several thousand years. (We've already covered Babylon, if only briefly.) There is no question that the Chinese — inventors of fireworks, al dente vegetables, MSG, and countless other major creations (as well as being the most capitalistic people in the world at this moment in history) — are a remarkable, admirable civilization. How interesting it is, then, that they have known for millennia that the contrarian approach is the wisest way to go.

I take, as Exhibit A, the Chinese written symbol for "crisis," which is pronounced "un-geh." There are two hieroglyphs, or characters, that make up that often-frightening word, each different. One says "Danger!" and the other says "Opportunity!"

Now, isn't that a most fascinating linkage of words? The Chinese equation is, to put it in mathematical form, extremely informative: Crisis = Danger + Opportunity. Who could argue with that? I, being non-Chinese, have my own, not-unrelated expression: Your attitude determines your altitude.

Let me put this another way: While most people — investors, especially — tend to focus on danger when they encounter a crisis, the true investor — the wise, thoughtful, and ultimately *successful* investor — focuses on opportunity.

What do I mean by this? That the successful investor actually welcomes volatility in the stock market, in the real estate market, and in every other situation, whereas that very up-and-down, uncertain situation is usually what sends the vast majority of investors focusing only on the danger aspect and heading for the hills to take cover (after stupidly dumping their stocks and mutuals just before they left town).

But not you, Dear Reader. You are aware, as the great Chinese people have been aware since before the time of Christ — indeed, from even before the Babylonians — that crisis often can be dangerous but that it inevitably carries with it great opportunity. Which is why you, from the moment you read this, will stop this idiotic, self-destructive (and, more relevantly, financially destructive) focusing on the danger in every crisis (be it stock market "correction" or even stock market "crash") and focus mainly on the opportunity that those crises offer. (As I've already noted, "your attitude determines your altitude." And you *do* wish to fly high with your investments and your future security, do you not?)

I talk a lot about the remarkable Berkshire Hathaway company in this book, and with good reason. During the Gulf War crisis (yes, there's that word again) of 1992, Mr. Warren Buffett's company fell from $8,900 a share to $5,600. My best friend, Graham Downer, who owns two McDonald's restaurants in Cambridge, Ontario, saw "opportunity" rather than "danger" in those falling share prices, and he purchased many shares at $5,600. (Even if he had done so at $8,800, my point remains.)

My friend must now feel great pleasure when he sees those same shares, just a few short years later, worth over $48,000 each. But think of the anguish and even the rage of the people who panicked and sold their Berkshire Hathaway shares at low prices, and now witness how this extraordinary company has shot back up, and beyond, in spades, clubs, diamonds, and aces. Where my buddy Graham saw "opportunity" in what was obviously a crisis in the market and in that majestic stock, countless others saw only the "danger," and they dumped their shares like you would a poisoned apple.

The *Globe and Mail* Report on Business interviewed my friend in the fall of 1996, and the article is well worth quoting at length, since his opinions capture so well what I am trying to teach in this book.

Forget Instant Gratification

Graham Downer has accumulated significant wealth by doing his bit to instantly satisfy the cravings of Canada's hungry. Now he's intent on making his portfolio grow by personally avoiding any temptation for instant financial gratification.

"The stock market is just too emotional and responds too much to things that don't have any meaning to the value of a company," says the 51-year-old owner of two McDonald's restaurants in his home town of Cambridge, Ont.

Mr. Downer says he became a long-term, buy-and-hold investor six years ago, and it's been rewarding him with stellar gains of 20 per cent to 25 per cent a year ever since. "I became a disciple of Warren Buffett and took what he says about buying and holding good companies to heart."

One of his very first long-term bets was mutual fund giant Trimark Financial Corp. "I bought it at around $12, and adjusted for splits it's probably around $150." . . .

Mr. Downer is also a keen buyer of mutual funds, which make up the bulk of his portfolio. He was an early investor in the AIC Advantage Fund, a Canadian equity fund that invests in shares of mutual fund managers and financial companies. He bought in at $12.42 a unit in 1991, and the units are now around $60.

The fund has a one-year return to Aug. 31 of just over 50 per cent, and a 10-year compound annual return of 14.2 per cent. He bought into the AIC Value Fund, a U.S. equity fund, in 1990 at $7.82. The units are now around $27.75. The fund has a five-year compound return of 19.2 per cent.

His returns are amplified by the use of borrowed money. One of his trading accounts is margined up to 20 per cent. He also has a leveraged account, funded by a bank loan, with the investments in the account serving as security. "I see it as optimizing opportunities to create wealth," he says.

Before his conversion to long-term investing, Mr. Downer admits having met his share of losses trying to pick overnight successes. "I was jumping in and out of the market using my heart, not my head," he says.

His worst move in recent years — buying Republic Waste Industries Inc. (controlled at the time by former Laidlaw Inc. chief Michael Degroote) in 1991 — was when he abandoned his buy-and-hold beliefs. "I went to this big hyped-up marketing meeting, and got all caught up in the excitement," he recalls. "I put in around $40,000 and it proceeded to go to half of that, and I sold it."

Still, he says, those occasional lapses renew his faith in the buy-and-hold approach. "I get burnt, shake myself and go back to what works."

His advice to others: "Buy companies with good management and good track records, and hold them for a long period of time," he says.

"My biggest advice is patience, patience, patience."

Along with a photograph of Graham is what newspaper people call a "sidebar," which includes other quotations from the investor. Under "best advice," my friend is quoted as declaring, "You have to be patient and not get emotional. You can't look at this stuff every day — it just drives you crazy." (I agree, and will have more to say about this later.)

What makes people panic? Why do some people put on boxing gloves while others turn tail? (I believe that scientists refer to this as the "fight or flight" response, and it may well be built into our nervous systems, going back millions of years.)

I certainly do not understand why so many people choose to "handle" crises or seeming disaster by selling off their best investments; that may well be for a registered psychiatrist to consider and explain. But I do know this much —

When there is a crisis, it is the best time in the world to invest. One should not fear it. On the contrary, it should be welcomed.

Why? you ask — and it's a perfectly understandable question. When stocks fall precipitously, is that not the time to "cut bait"? To "save what you can"? To "get out while the getting is good"? (It's not by chance that there are so many clichés about this action; it's a very popular — if not particularly clever — road to take. And, most assuredly, it is a road very much travelled, indeed.)

I'll tell you why not: Because when there *is* a crisis — be it war in the Gulf, Quebec threatening to separate, the death of a political leader, tensions in the Middle East (you name it; there are plenty of new ones to choose from, every single day) — it is inevitably accompanied by wonderful opportunities.

What kind of wonderful opportunities? To buy up great stocks at low prices. To buy good businesses. To start your own business. To purchase real estate. To buy *any* asset at low, discount prices. (Or maybe you always prefer to pay full price?)

But that's not the way that the masses act, is it? No, they behave irresponsibly and irrationally — and the key word here is the latter, irrationally — and sell off great investments or quality businesses at absurd prices! And we really do know why, don't we? Because they see only the Chinese character for "danger," and they ignore the same-sized word "opportunity" hidden in that same scary word — crisis.

As you can see, being a contrarian is crucial, because it always tells you the wisest time to invest: when others are heading for the Exit doors.

You know the ones who are painting the word "EXIT" in larger and brighter letters every single day, don't you?: the newspapers and magazines. Most people, alas, get much of their investment knowledge from the daily paper. And the majority of newspapers tell people such uninspired (and jump-on-the-bandwagon) things as how we should all "invest now" — or soon after everyone else has done so; true, the price of those shares is high, but then, that's because they are so hot! (And to think that we humans actually feel superior to lemmings, as they follow each into the sea!)

It is to laugh — or to weep. While the great stock market cliché is "buy low, sell high!" it seems as if the entire world has conspired to urge us to "buy high!" (when everyone else is buying, and pushing those shares up in price), and only then to "sell low!" (as you panic and hurry to dump your shares, terrified by the inevitable newspaper headlines that scream "Market Tumbles for Second Straight Day!").

My attitude — and *alti*tude, if I say so myself — is similar to that of Warren Buffett and Berkshire Hathaway: If you can, buy low and (much, much later) sell high. And even if you can't buy low, then at least buy excellent businesses at reasonable prices — and then hold on to them. (And *don't* dump them at the first sign of market hysteria, which is, alas, inevitable.)

All this discussion of crises brings me to the topic of market timing, which is the subject of many a book. It's very informative that there are no billionaires in the Forbes Four Hundred Richest People listings who are market timers; they are all prudent business owners! I don't really know of any individuals who have made money on market timing, because they will inevitably make an incorrect move and give back the money, sooner or later. It's all guesswork; it's all garbage.

Not so the contrarian investor! He or she *knows* that the best prices to be had are when markets are going through turmoil! You don't have to look back any further, at least in

Canada, than the days following the ill-fated Meech Lake accord, or the Charlottetown accord (or was it discord?), or the squeaky-close Quebec referendum of 1995. In the U.S., it can be anything from political assassination to Senate scandal to race riots to international war jitters.

I'll say this several times in this book, but it bears repeating: Meech Lake may collapse, but billions of people will still reach for a Coke the following day. The Charlottetown accord may fall apart, but billions will still have to shave the next morning with a Gillette razor, to paraphrase that keen insight from Mr. Buffett. True, the fine Canadian firm of Bombardier is located in the province of Quebec, but you don't need to possess a doctorate in political science to know that if Quebec becomes hostile, or, sadly, even if it becomes independent, that company will simply pick up and move elsewhere, seeking out a friendlier environment. And no amount of failed constitutional conferences or even independent provinces will prevent people, whether they be Canadian, American, or European, from buying their Ski-Doos, Jet Skis, corporate aircraft, and the many other superior products that Bombardier manufactures, markets, and sells so brilliantly. And the most dreadful political upheavals in the United States, the U.K., or Europe will not prevent the average man or woman in each country from pulling on their Levi's jeans, sliding into their Nike shoes, and heading off to grab a hamburger and soft drink at their nearest McDonald's.

No, what the contrarian cares about is the earnings of each business, not external crises, which, more often than not, go away as surely as morning dew. The true contrarian is an opportunist who recognizes that every crisis produces not only danger. And rather than be negative, the true contrarian focuses on the opportunity that invariably presents itself at the same, difficult time.

Indeed, this problem of "predicting the market" is worth a section all its own.

It's Not Timing the Market — It's Time *in* the Market

Timing can be crucial, if you are a married couple who wishes to conceive a child, or a basketball team with a two-point lead (or deficit) with 10 seconds to go in the fourth quarter of the game.

But one thing I am forever telling my clients is this: It is impossible to predict the stock market. And even if we could, it is ultimately irrelevant! And by irrelevant, I mean precisely that. *Predicting the market is totally, completely, 100% irrelevant.*

I talk about Coca-Cola a lot in this book, but I don't do this because it happens to make up such a large percentage of Warren Buffett's Berkshire Hathaway portfolio. Please recall what I mentioned earlier about Coke's share-price movement over the past several years — from the year 1980, to be precise. Since that year, the common stock of Coca-Cola has grown by an average of 28% per annum. And don't forget that an investment of $100,000 in Coca-Cola shares in that year would grow to become, by the summer of 1997, over $5.5 million!

(And, since you may not have had $100,000 to invest some 17 years ago, then try it this way: If you had invested a mere $10,000 in shares of Coke in 1980, you'd now be in the possession of over half a million dollars. Still pretty impressive.)

But I'm not talking here about What You Should Have Done; I'm talking about the absurdity of Trying to Predict the Market. Since you (and I) failed to make that brilliant investment in Coca-Cola, a lot has happened in the world: The federal government of Canada has gone from Liberal to Conservative to Liberal; the presidency of the United States has see-sawed from Democratic to Republican to Democratic; the federal deficits of both countries have skyrocketed; there have been constant political crises in the former Soviet Union, the Middle East, and Africa; totalitarian governments have fallen across Eastern Europe and Russia, as did the Berlin Wall (adding several million thirsty mouths and faces for Coke and Gillette products); there was a frightening — or was it? — "stock market crash" in Canada, the United States, and around the globe in the fall of 1987; and interest rates have gone from towering, even usurious heights down to the lowest numbers in half a century (at least in the spring of 1997, as I write these words).

To paraphrase a famous banking song, "The times, they've been a-changin'."

Yes, the world *has* changed quite a bit since 1980, has it not? Yet did you come across many newspaper or magazine articles that predicted any of these crises? Neither did I. All they did was report what happened in the world — *after* it happened.

Yet all the while that the U.S.S.R. was shattering into a dozen pieces; that Romania's long-time dictator was tortured and then shot by his former subjects; that Israel invaded Lebanon, had its prime minister assassinated and several of its public buses blown up; that all of us shuddered (and probably dumped our stocks by the billions of shares) as the market fell so "precipitously" in October 1987; that O.J. Simpson did (or didn't) murder his wife and her friend — Coca-Cola shares continued to climb almost inexorably upward (with the occasional "correction," of course), by an average of some 28% *every single frightening, unsure, hit-and-miss, unpredictable year*!

Nostradamus did a pretty impressive job, back in the Middle Ages, mystically and mysteriously predicting world wars, assassinations, and social upheavals that would not occur until many centuries after he died, but I wouldn't play the market by his writings, any more than by the scribblings of the most esteemed "stock market timer."

No individual has the ability to successfully predict the future. Therefore, we should not pay any attention whatsoever to things over which we have no control!

No — I take that back. I'd like to now make a fearless prediction — and I can be far more confident of the correctness of *my* prediction than any Nostradamus or Jeanne Dixon of the past, present, or future: I here predict that the earnings of Coca-Cola will continue to grow, and will be much greater by the first year of the next millennium, 2001, than they are in the summer of 1997.

Now, how can I possibly make such a fearless, reckless prediction? Well, because in the countries where 650 million people live, Coca-Cola sells over 150 million soft drink servings every year. Yet in the areas where another 3.6 billion people live, Coca-Cola sells less than 10 soft drink servings each year.

And how about India, which is closing in on one billion people? In poor, overcrowded India, Coke sells *less than two*. And ever-more-affluent China, with its 1.3 billion and counting? Also less than two servings per person each year.

My heavens! What if our Indian friends start to drink 4 or 8 servings a year? What if our Chinese neighbours start to drink 5, 10, 20, even 50 servings a year?

Dear Reader, there are so many things that could happen over the coming decade(s). Hurricanes, floods, and earthquakes. Peace could break out in the Middle East. All those Serbs and Croats and Bosnians could all reunite in a joyously resurrected Yugoslavia. Well, maybe not *that*.

Inarguably, anything and everything is possible in the future.

But I *can* tell you what is probable: that there will be a dramatic rise in the value of Coca-Cola shares so huge that our heads will collectively spin. Of course, there will always be those shareholders — probably 90% of them — who will far too eagerly sell their shares over the next few years, happily "taking their profits," but thereby giving up the potential of seeing their savings/investments double, triple, and even more. And at an average of 28% increase in Coca-Cola's share prices every year since 1980 — and without the thirst of over 2 billion-plus people in China and the Indian subcontinent — it won't be taking very long for that doubling, tripling, and even more to occur, as it has consistently done in the past.

Which brings me back to this essential point: no one can predict the market. No one. But with a little bit of research into quality businesses, you can do rather well — providing that you are not self-destructive with your investment decisions. (More on that below.)

Being a contrarian means that you must be passionately

committed to three major beliefs — all of which, interestingly, radiate more common sense than 90% of all non-contrarian investors. Here they are, one by one.

1. You *must* be a business owner!

And I mean be a business owner, regardless of what you actually "do" in your life and career. If you are currently running a business (whether bike repair or baking bread, that's not my concern), then you have already achieved this. It is not by chance that, in every part of the world, the richest people are those who own businesses.

But even if you do not see yourself as a "business owner," you become one when you invest in common stocks. So, if you are a civil servant, own a business (or at least a tiny chunk of a business, through shares in a company you trust). If you are a doctor, do the same. Or a teacher. Even if you are an unemployed labourer, somehow find the money (more on that, as well, below) and do it.

You *must* have commitment to business ownership if you wish to grow and prosper. (And buying and selling shares in countless different companies, jumping from ownership to ownership like a kangaroo on steroids, is not what I am talking about here.)

2. Make sure that you own an excellent business with wonderful, long-term economic fundamentals.

Every business, much like every person, is not necessarily decent, reliable, trustworthy, and has growth potential. So what I'm talking about here is obvious: When you "own" (i.e., invest in) a business, you should own only those that are domiciled in strong, long-term growth industries, and run by honest shareowner-oriented managements.

3. Your share-ownership in that business you "own" should be *permanent!*

I do not mean permanent in the way that your hair-dresser does, since those permanents usually last only a few days or weeks. I mean precisely the opposite of what 95% of all "players" in the stock markets and mutual funds do. You must actually buy and hold your "ownership" of that business (or businesses) in the way that most of our grandparents married, and truly believed in the words of the preacher: "For better or for worse, for richer or poorer, in sickness and in health . . ." This metaphor works surprisingly well, because what business has not had its better days and its worse days; which business has not been richer on some days and poorer on others; which business has never been sick and/or healthy?

The fantastic success of Warren Buffett, and other great investors to whom I refer in this book, is due not so much to what they have done as to what they have *not* done.

They have *not* sold their investments.

They have *not* taken any profits.

They have *not* been flitting from stock to stock to stock like a starving bumblebee or butterfly.

These men and women never say, "Look! The market is high this week! I'd better sell my shares now, because the market will undoubtedly fall, and I can always buy back in!"

These people have done the simplest thing possible, not unlike a business owner who nurtures his business through good times and bad, by paying careful attention to the fundamentals. They have purchased quality businesses (or shares in them), and held on for the long haul, because they had faith in the worth of those businesses — and *not* gone for the immediate gratification of making a killing on the stock market. And who of us has not heard a friend say, "Guess how well I did! I bought a thousand shares of X at $XX just a few months ago, and I just dumped them at $XXX, for a profit of $XXXXX! Not bad, eh?"

Actually, I think it's plenty bad, and terribly risky, and pretty stupid — and this book will show you why this is so.

Now it's time for one of my favourite analogies, which I heard from one of the great investors whom I respect and admire. I sense he'll forgive the paraphrase: "Keep your eyes focused on the playing field!"

What do I mean by this? It's simple and logical, really. Imagine that you and a friend have gone to a game — baseball, football, basketball, hockey, whatever. Your friend keeps his eyes firmly fastened on the scoreboard.

"Look, we're ahead!" he says at one point.

"Oh, no! We've fallen behind!" comes later.

"Look at the score now! We're *never* gonna catch up!"

And so on, ad nauseam.

Your friend — who may be a very good friend and a fine husband and father — is an idiot, at least in this situation. You are both attending a competition, and all the important, crucial action — the stuff that counts — is right out there on the diamond, the playing field, the court, the ice. And your buddy has chosen to keep his eyes firmly fixed on that stupid scoreboard!

This analogy makes a tremendous amount of sense, does it not? When one goes to a sports event, one does not spend all one's time focused on the scoreboard. One should — nay, *must* — look at the playing field, because what's happening on that playing field is what eventually puts the numbers up on the scoreboard! Of course we all like to look up at the scoreboard — occasionally — to see who's ahead, who's behind. But it is obviously the playing field where all eyes should be riveted.

If you haven't figured out the connection by now, here it is in living black and white: The stock market is the scoreboard! And the playing field is the businesses themselves!

Now, when you are investing in publicly-traded securities or mutual funds, it's nice to know — occasionally — how they are doing, but you certainly want to spend very little of your time staring at the stock market pages/scoreboard! They are irrelevant.

It is what is happening to the business — its profits and losses, its sales and its breakthroughs and its setbacks and its plans for the future — that is truly important, and that *is* the playing field.

Naturally (to continue the analogy), the man or woman who knows the batting average of a particular baseball player against a certain pitcher, or against left-handed or right-handed pitchers, or how well he hits when there are men on base, and his strike-out percentages, has a lot more fun at the ballpark than the person (or politician) who believes that the Dodgers are still in Brooklyn.

The same with the thoughtful person who keeps his or

her eyes on the business/playing field. One should do every-thing possible to further understand the business, through attending shareholder meetings, reading annual reports, following management machinations and plans. To ignore how a business is doing (or to not watch the players on the field) is to endanger one's investment, not to mention pleasure. A business owner (i.e., investor in a business or businesses) *must* pay attention to the business funda-mentals, and not focus on the often silly, usually irrational movements of the stock market. (After all, most investors are self-destructive and greedy, as we know so well, usually from personal experience.)

A brief example of the scoreboard/playing field analogy, linked with a major Canadian business, could be helpful here. I sense that most of you are familiar with Magna International, the magnificently successful auto-parts maker, co-founded and built into a billion-dollar firm by Frank Stronach. The stock price of Magna began to fall like a stone several years ago, after Mr. Stronach stepped down, even though the company continued to put several hundreds of dollars in parts into every single car built in North America. One week it sold for over $30 (on the scoreboard known as the Toronto Stock Exchange); within months it had dropped to, and hovered around, the $2 range.

Investors dumped Magna shares by the millions — and who could blame them? They watched the scoreboard/stock market pages daily; they saw their investment crumbling like Miss Havisham's wedding cake. Yet Magna *continued* to manufacture auto parts by the tens of millions, and sales *continued* to grow around the world.

Stronach came back and took over the reins of his

beloved company once again, and the stock began to shoot up in a surprisingly short period of time: $4, $8, $20, $40 — up to over $85 in June 1997. Those who watched only the scoreboard got badly burned; those who kept their eyes on the playing field (Magna's sales, its factories, its expansion, its leader's return to the running of the company) did quite a bit better, wouldn't you agree?

This leads me to one further point about the success of the contrarian approach.

Leave Self-Destruction to the *Mission: Impossible* Tape

Even if you don't recall the popular TV show of several decades ago, *Mission: Impossible*, the chances are pretty good that you saw the recent box-office-smash movie of the same name, starring Tom Cruise. (By the way, he also produced it, which is why he made over $30 million from the film, rather than his usual salary of less than half that. How's that for a further example of the importance of owning your own business?) There was a memorable line in both, which went like this: "Your mission, should you choose to take it, is . . ." after which the voice concluded, "This tape will self-destruct in five seconds." Suddenly, smoke would pour out of the tape recorder, and no one but our hero and several million television or movie viewers knew precisely what that top-secret (and never-quite-impossible) mission was.

I mention this here because one of the major purposes of the contrarian approach to investing is, it keeps you, the stock/mutual fund/business-owner, from self-destructing like that doomed little cassette tape used in *Mission: Impossible*.

One of the worst, most treacherous clichés in the world of investing is "buy low and sell high." This is nonsense, and it never works consistently. Even worse, it leads to Las Vegas–type gambling, and not the true investing that I am urging throughout this book. The line should actually read, "buy and hold."

People forget that the only way to get stocks when they are truly low-priced is when there is a crisis (and you have not forgotten already, I trust, my Chinese equation of Crisis = Danger + Opportunity). War breaks out in an oil-producing country? Ten million oranges freeze on the trees of central Florida? Something is always happening to make investors panic (and, yes, to self-destruct), which allows us brilliant contrarians to leap in and "buy low."

The key to being a contrarian is to recognize that you are only going to get a truly "good" price when other people are selling. And you already know why they are selling like mad: because of their own irrational (read self-destructive) behaviour. Those poor souls (and we've all been one of them, let's face it) are dumping their securities at foolishly low prices because they are terrified that their net worth will drop to zero. And, to be honest, who can blame them for reacting irrationally and self-destructively? It's hard to hold on to a ship when it seems to be sinking, and rather rapidly at that. And the water is so very cold . . .

But if you have been investing in an excellent, quality, top-notch, well-positioned (feel free to reach for a thesaurus and fill in your own adjective) business, you don't have to worry, do you? Of course, stock markets and stock prices and mutual funds will fluctuate, often even hourly, but over time nothing on the face of the earth will ever give you what a superior publicly-traded security will give you, with the possible exception of your own personally run business.

Ever notice what happens in the newspapers and magazines when the stock market suddenly turns bearish? The headlines never read "Now Is the Time to Invest!" do they? No, they read "Banks Mired in Depression!" "Trust Companies Fear Bankruptcy!" "Businesses Expect Dreadful Future in Crumbling Marketplace!" "Stocks Fall Faster than Michael Jackson's Reputation!" and similar bons mots.

I remember reading headlines like these during the major recession of the early 1980s, and once again, through late October and November 1987. And I also remember what most people have long forgotten, that even in that frightening, death-defying year of '87, the average stock on the Standard & Poor's 500 *still* rose over 5% over those 12 months — and then continued to rise another 16% or more in the following 12 months! Some Crash. Some Great Depression.

Mr. Templeton, the admirable founder of one of the most successful collections of mutual funds of all time, once exclaimed, "Don't ask me where the outlook is good; ask me where it's the worst." He went on to add, "You see, it's where the outlook is worst, and when blood is in the streets, that one is going to get the very best prices. Because when you are dealing with publicly-traded securities, you're trying to buy at the very best price. And that will come only when there are bad times."

I shall now call upon my wonderful Jamaican heritage for a classic aphorism: "Chicken merry, hawk near!" You get the picture: A chicken runs out into the farmyard, sunning her feathers, feeling euphoric and enjoying the great weather, and, inevitably, the hawk will be nearby, ready to pounce.

And that's precisely — if less poetically — what we heard throughout the fall and winter of 1996/97, as people grew euphoric about the returns they had on their mutual funds and stocks, and how the stock market has been on a tear since 1992, and the Dow Jones soared past 6,000 for the first time in history. Chicken merry, hawk near! you hear from everyone. When will it all come crashing down? When should we "get out" of this dangerously over-heated market? When will the hawk come swooping?

When, indeed.

I'm talking about self-destructive attitudes here. As I've noted, attitude determines one's altitude, and fear of poverty too often makes that poverty a reality. It is rotten attitudes (uh-oh, hawk near!) that hold so many of us back from seeing the opportunity, whether in the crisis or even in the chicken-merry times.

Was it Mark Twain or Stephen Leacock who wrote that "when opportunity knocks, most people are off in a bar, drinking beer"? But even if they *do* hear that knocking when they are home, intensely perusing the stock market page (and ignoring the playing field), they often think, "It's too good to be true; it can't be happening to me; can it really be Ed McMahon from the Publishers Clearing House at the door, clutching a $10-million cheque with my name on it?" (Well, probably not.)

People are simply self-destructive with their investment decisions. They don't like paying reasonable prices; they actually feel better and more clever when they are paying higher prices (!). I often ask my clients to view their investments in the same way that they view their supermarket shopping. In other words, when you look at the stock market, think *supermarket.*

When there is a great sale on toilet paper — eight rolls for the price of six! — do we not tend to stock up? You know we do. When there is an exciting deal on your favourite canned soup, or canned beans, or potato chips, don't you buy as many as they will let you buy? You bet. (Sales on milk or yoghurt or something perishable are different, of course, but I still see many people stocking up on ice cream when there's a great deal being offered.)

And why *do* nearly all of us stock up on toilet paper and canned goods at our friendly neighbourhood supermarket when there is a sale on, or a 40%-off coupon available through the mail or in the daily newspaper? We all know why: there is great pleasure that comes from looking into our pantry and declaring, if only to ourselves, "I paid $1.29 a box for that facial tissue only last month! And here I just managed to buy a dozen boxes for only 79 cents each! How proud Mother would be if she could see me saving money like this!" It's almost visceral, this feeling of "I got a real bargain," and it's perfectly logical. After all, who likes to waste money?

The latter is not a rhetorical question, since it has a very troubling answer. Tens of millions of men and women must love to waste money, because they display this habit every single day on the stock markets of the world!

You want further examples of absurd, self-destructive behaviour? Of manic behaviour — which quickly leads to depressive feelings of near-despair?

Look no further than the price of gold! Remember how gold was artificially "fixed" at $35 an ounce for many decades, until it was finally freed from those constraints? It shot up — literally overnight — to $100 an ounce, $300, $500, even $800 an ounce. And when did the largest number of people leap into this doomed-to-crash hysteria? When gold hit a grotesque $900 an ounce, at which point men and women were lined up by the thousands along Bay Street in Toronto and Wall Street in New York taking out mortgages on their houses, so eager they were to leap on the boat when it was actually leaving the harbour.

We all know what happened; the price of gold collapsed like a cheap suitcase, and millions were wiped out. And it has rarely (if ever) broken $400 an ounce over the two decades since — during which time, countless stocks of great, trustworthy companies have skyrocketed in value and price.

Here's another self-destructive tale, and one that is a lot closer to home for Canadian readers: People lined up by the thousands to buy condominiums from various builders across Canada, right through the late 1980s, especially in Toronto, when some real estate was reaching $400 a square foot.

They sure aren't lining up now, are they? You can pick one up, like an over-ripe apple from a tree, for 50% less than those peak prices today, in the late-1990s. Just don't mention what you paid for it to your still-suffering next-door neighbour, who purchased his condo at the peak of the market, just before the whole thing crashed. Imagine how his still-broken heart would shatter further when he realizes that he's still got a $250,000 mortgage on that gorgeous condo, after putting up an equal amount in cash when the market was so hot (and would clearly keep on going up forever), while you didn't put a penny down and have a mortgage of only 200 grand. But then, who ever said that life was fair? (As a witty caption reads under an advertisement of a beautiful SL500 Mercedes: "If life was fair, we'd all have one of these.")

The answer, of course, is to *never* jump on the bandwagon, whether that bandwagon is plugging gold, condos, or "hot" stocks. The true contrarian must view publicly-traded securities as investments, not as paper to be shuffled and quickly traded or dumped. One must avoid getting involved with manias, which is the ultimate in self-destructiveness.

But what do I mean when I write "mania"? After all, many thoughtful people have claimed that the entire mutual fund "boom" is a mania!

I beg to differ. Because unlike gold, condos, or tulip bulbs in Holland several centuries ago, mutual funds are not a "thing," they are a system of investing. And this system of investing has grown along with a powerful demographic shift from consumption to saving in North America, as the aging Baby Boomer population has become convinced that their governments will probably never be able to provide them with an adequate pension — as their parents had believed, and, in most cases, had received.

Remember that best-selling book earlier this decade called *Rotten Men and the Women Who Tolerate Them*, or something like that? Well, if I wanted to be truly cynical and negative, I could well call this book *Self-Destructive People and the Lousy Investment Decisions They Make*. But that would be too negative, and I'm always plugging how very important it is to be positive in one's life and one's attitudes.

So let's just conclude my Third Law of Wealth by saying, if one follows the contrarian approach in purchasing shares of businesses on the stock market (as we do every week almost unconsciously at the supermarket), we will do best if we keep our eye on the playing field (and not on the scoreboard/stock market pages), purchase only quality businesses (or portions thereof), avoid manias, and stop being so dreadfully self-destructive.

And now, on to Rule Four.

8

Fourth Law:
Leverage Human Resources

INTERESTINGLY, just as most people are contrarian at the *super*market (always eager to purchase consumer products at low prices), if not in the *stock* market, the majority of humanity is already steeped in this philosophy, if only unconsciously.

The examples come easily. You have a mechanical problem with your automobile. It keeps stalling; it's making strange and unwelcome noises; it consumes far too much gas. Do you fix it yourself? (Some do, but few of us have the ability, what with today's increasingly complex computerized cars.) No, you hire a competent mechanic, whose job it is to know what's wrong, to find it quickly, and repair it.

Legal problem? It may drive you crazy, but you sense that it'll drive you even crazier unless you turn to a lawyer.

Let's talk actual life and death for a moment. You

suddenly have chest pains (heaven forbid). Do you take a course in open-heart surgery at your nearby community college or Learning Annex?

I sense not. Most of us are reluctant to take out our own hearts and fix them ourselves; indeed, this same ready-acceptance of "going to the experts" is why we tend to turn to social workers, psychologists, and psychiatrists when we encounter family or emotional difficulties. We know, almost instinctively, that we want experts to fix our car, our legal problems, and our health, whether physical or mental. All of us have witnessed our own parents call a plumber or electrician when they felt they could not deal with the dilemma themselves, and we respected them for it; after all, what are professionals (and craftspeople) for, if not to fix or improve or heal what we ourselves cannot accomplish with as much skill, speed, or simple ability?

As I said, my Rule Number Four of Wealth is actually part of the unconscious way that we tend to do things in our lives. Yet when it comes to personal investment, financial planning, and wealth creation — so that we do not leave that 65- or 70-year-old who lives in us all up the financial creek when he or she suddenly appears before us — how many of us "leverage" *this* human resource? Sadly, far too few, and the results are often tragic.

Who Is on Your Board of Directors?

Just as we turn to a medical doctor for our ills, it is essential that we turn to experts in financial dealings for our monetary present and future. I like to put it to my clients this way: "Take a businesslike approach to your personal affairs, and actually establish a board of directors!" (In other words, leverage those human resources.)

Every major company has a board of directors, and the purpose of that board is singular and essential: How can we best bring independent thinking to management meetings, to explore ways to maximize shareholders' wealth? Down at the board meetings in Atlanta, Georgia, the board of directors of Coca-Cola has Warren Buffett sitting there, along with Peter V. Ueberroth, the president of the Sun Trust Bank of Atlanta, and many others — all of them bringing their insights and advice as to how that company can continue to thrive. I can assure you, their president, Robert Gouizctta, listens open-mindedly and eagerly to his board of directors, and it's not only because they each happen to be wealthy enough or lucky enough to own a large number of Coca-Cola shares.

In the world of personal finance, you will want to establish your own board of directors. And to take a businesslike approach, you need to surround yourself with the best thinkers and the finest financial advice available. You will therefore wish to align yourself only with those who have proven investment strategies. By electing a personal investment advisor to become your own chairman of the board, he or she will bring to you other areas of expertise and professionals in the field, along with money managers, and so on. Your automobile deserves the finest mechanic, your health the finest doctor — and your financial portfolio the finest experts and investment advisors.

Once again: Just as you would be wise to refrain from performing your own open-heart surgery, similarly you should never take a two-week course on investment strategies and then go and do it yourself. Or go to a no-load discount broker. No, you should demand a powerful investment advisor as chairman of your board of directors, who will direct you wisely and thoughtfully, and keep you invested in a portfolio of superb, successful businesses for the rest of your life. I believe that it is improbable that one can put into place, and keep together, a quality investment program over a lifetime, without some help from a professional investment advisor.

Not unrelated to the above, here is the Fifth Law of Wealth.

9

Fifth Law:

Leverage Capital

THIS law is the one that frightens people the most, so let me attempt to allay your fears with a far-more-frightening declaration: it is impossible to work, pay taxes, and save your after-tax income and *still* manage to build up a meaningful net worth. It is simply too small an amount to begin accumulating serious money. Even when you use your RRSP to its fullest degree — which is tax-deferred, of course — your nest egg is going to be insufficient.

I cannot deny that this last law of mine is quite controversial, but being controversial does not mean that it has to be risky: *One must borrow money in order to invest* and build a suitable nest egg that will serve for the retirement of someone with greater needs than a bird.

Before you begin to panic and close this book, think about the house in which many of you now dwell. How did you purchase that home? If you are like the vast majority of citizens of this country, indeed, of this world, you took out a mortgage to be able to afford it.

Now, most people tend to view home ownership as an investment, but this is simply not so. It is a lifestyle choice. And you would never be living in your present house had you not borrowed the money to buy it. In much the same way, unless you borrow money to invest, you are probably not going to have an adequate net worth.

What's almost funny about this law is, the vast majority of Canadians are incredibly eager to borrow billions of dollars to purchase consumer durables! Indeed, as I write these words in the summer of 1997, there is close to $500 billion in consumer debt in this country. Debt on credit cards. On car loans. On still-unpaid-for fridges and stoves. On houses.

On Owning a House, or Reaching for a Coke

Many of you will not like it when I say this, but it's true: home ownership is inarguably the *single greatest detriment* to wealth creation in North America. The average home owner, in slowly paying off a mortgage of several hundred thousand dollars, ends up spending close to a million dollars in payments over several decades! Once again, home owner-ship is *not* an investment; it's simply where (and how) you choose to live. And it is a utility, and *not* wealth creation!

This will be a painful example, but I must give it. Think of the person who borrowed $100,000 as a down-payment on a house in 1980, and his friend, who borrowed the same sum to purchase shares in Coca-Cola. You already know about what happened to the latter; it's worth several million dollars today, which could buy a half-dozen houses in several locations around the world, most of them a lot warmer than Canada.

And the house "owner"? His house probably has gone up in value — maybe even two or three times. Let's say five times, just to be generous to the poor guy. So, he now owns a house (well, he undoubtedly still has a way to go on the mortgage) that's worth half a million dollars. Big deal.

Which situation would you rather be in today? Which person did better?

My point was illustrated quite brilliantly by a journalist named Josh McHugh in the June 19, 1995, issue of *Forbes* magazine. The one-page article was wittily entitled "Why the Kennedys Aren't the Rockefellers," and here is essentially what it said:

Most of us were pretty impressed when the Kennedys sold their famous beachfront home in Palm Beach, Florida, for $4.9 million that year; after all, the family patriarch Joe Kennedy had paid only $100,000 for it, six decades earlier!

A fifty-fold increase in the value of the house, most of us thought to ourselves. *What a great deal.*

But trust a clever journalist to discover the truth. When you reach for a calculator, you quickly realize that Joe Kennedy's $100,000, sunk into that lovely house and property in 1933, actually grew at a compound annual rate of only 6.5% over those 62 years in order to reach the $4.9-million sale price!

To quote from the *Forbes* article: "That's about two percentage points ahead of inflation over the six decades, but it lags behind even the price appreciation of the S&P 500. We exclude here dividends on the S&P 500 (as well as taxes and upkeep on the house)."

Ahh, but what if Joe Kennedy had put the same $100,000 into Standard Oil of New Jersey stock in the same year? It "would have compounded at more than 13% annually — and now be worth about $250 million in Exxon stock. Today the Rockefellers are billionaires on The Forbes Four Hundred. The centimillionaire Kennedys barely made the list last year [1994] and may not make it this year."

The journalist's conclusion? "Houses are nice to live in, but if you want to leave your heirs serious money, buy common stocks, and . . . reinvest those dividends."

Borrowing need not be scary; many individuals have borrowed money to be able to start a business. Most of us borrow to purchase houses and cars. So why not borrow money to invest thoughtfully, carefully, and creatively? (Especially when one follows the first four of my rules: Pay yourself first. Set articulated financial goals. Be a contrarian by ignoring the stock market and taking the road less travelled. Leverage human resources. And, of course, this fifth one — use other people's money to make more money for yourself, your retirement, your children, your future.)

As I was creating this chapter, I was interviewed at length (in the fall of 1996) by a fine journalist from Canada's largest newspaper, *The Toronto Star*. Jade Hemeon, whose column "Mutual Funds" appears regularly, articulated my feelings about this fifth and crucial rule so well that I asked her permission to quote in full that article, which ran in that paper on October 27 of that year. It captures my views perfectly.

When Borrowing to Invest Makes Some Sense

With interest rates lower than they've been since the 1950s, the idea of borrowing to invest is worth considering.

Many people steer away from taking out a loan to buy mutual funds or shares for fear of risk. But the strategy should be weighed in a dispassionate manner.

After all, home buyers take on big mortgages to purchase an asset that produces *no* income and is often a money pit.

Others will borrow to invest in their own businesses — often a risky start-up venture. [Author's note: Indeed, four out of five new businesses fail within their first five years of existence, which are pretty frightening odds, wouldn't you say?]

Why, then, doesn't it make sense to borrow to invest in carefully selected, diversified mutual funds or companies with conservative management and superior track records?

The key is to take a long-term perspective and borrow a manageable amount, with interest payments you can easily handle. Plunging into debt up to your neck to invest in speculative securities is financial suicide, but borrowing to invest in companies with proven success is a completely different strategy.

"One of the most important laws of wealth creation is that you must use other people's money to create a nest egg of any size," says Richard Charlton, senior vice-president at Fortune Financial. "With interest rates so low, borrowing makes more sense than ever."

The key, says Charlton, is to invest in the right public companies and the right mutual funds. He points to the long-term track records of consistent top performers such as Templeton Growth Fund, with a 10-year average annual return of 12 per cent, AIC Advantage Fund, with an average of 15.5 per cent over 10 years, and Trimark Fund, with 15.0 per cent.

While there are no ironclad guarantees that past returns will be repeated, a long track record is an indication that a fund manager can perform well through various types of market conditions.

With the prime rate at 5.25 per cent [as of the fall of 1996], floating-rate investment loans are available from such institutions as Canada Trust and the Bank of Montreal for as low as prime plus one-half a percentage point. The terms of loans depend on an individual's net worth, collateral and duration of the loan.

Unlike the interest on mortgages used to buy a home, the interest on an investment loan is tax deductible against income from investments. If investments don't pay enough in the form of interest or dividends to cover the loan cost, it is deductible against other income.

Stock mutual funds typically don't pay out a lot of interest and dividends, but provide the opportunity for capital gain. Capital gains are taxable in the year in which they are realized, but at a lower rate than interest and income. Capital gains taxes can be deferred by holding on to stocks for the long term, or selecting mutual funds with low portfolio turnover.

If you are in the top tax bracket, you can cut your actual after-tax interest costs by as much as half, because of the tax deductibility of interest. That could bring the after-tax cost of a 6 per cent loan as low as 3 per cent. For this strategy to succeed, your mutual funds returns need only be higher than your after-tax interest costs.

Investors must keep in mind that stocks and stock funds are volatile, and will have good years and bad. There could be some years when interest costs could exceed your investment returns. If you borrow to invest you must have the intestinal fortitude to withstand stock market corrections.

Charlton says investors must learn to view their stock investments or mutual funds in the same way as they would the purchase of a business. The idea is to buy securities for the long term, not for short-term trading profits.

Over the years, he has recommended such stocks as Gillette Co., Coca-Cola Co., Berkshire Hathaway, Trimark Investment Management, and the Canadian banks to his clients, as well as mutual funds where the managers practise a similar philosophy of buying superior businesses for the long term.

When you hold a good business, or a fund portfolio of good businesses, you are better able to resist the urge to panic and dump your holdings when the market corrects, Charlton says.

Borrowing to invest — known as leveraging — has its detractors. Among them is mutual fund guru John Templeton who is concerned about what's known as the margin call. A margin call occurs when you have pledged your stocks and mutual funds as collateral against a loan, and the terms of that loan require a minimum percentage of equity against debt.

If your investments fall drastically in value — reducing the value of your equity — you could be on the hook for more collateral to satisfy your lender. If you can't supply it, you could be forced to sell your investments in a down market.

Charlton advises his clients to minimize the risk by arranging a long-term investment loan with a lender, not short-term margin financing.

Some lenders are willing to provide long-term investment loans up to 20 years in maturity. Your mutual funds are used as collateral, but without the margin requirements — providing you have the ability to make payments and are a good credit risk. You can also borrow against a stable asset such as a fully paid-for home. If you're borrowing to invest in stocks or funds, your interest costs are tax deductible.

A 20-year investment loan of $50,000 could be arranged at today's interest rates to provide you with payments of $240 or so a month.

Tax deductibility would reduce these interest costs significantly. But only the interest portion of a loan payment is tax deductible, and the amount of principal in the payment rises as the loan ages.

If interest rates go up, a floating rate loan could become more expensive and you might find yourself facing higher payments than originally negotiated. But you can also make lump-sum payments to reduce the loan size before maturity.

Charlton says paying off a loan can be viewed in the same way as setting aside a monthly sum for savings purposes or making a regular monthly mutual fund contribution with an automatic deduction from your bank account — something many financial planners recommend. Instead of automatically saving $200 or $300 a month, you can use the same money as a loan payment. The key is to borrow only an amount which you can afford to carry in the long term and where your financial well-being will not be jeopardized if your investments don't work out as planned.

"The biggest impediment to borrowing is fear," Charlton says. "But people should allow intelligence to rule their behavior."

Investing, let alone borrowing to invest, is still a new idea to many Canadians who have traditionally let their savings sit in guaranteed annual investment certificates and who are tied to the sense of security of owning their own bricks and mortar.

But many older people who have homes are finding they can't live on the income currently provided by GICs. They haven't built up an adequate financial nest egg to pay their living costs and are forced into such unhappy alternatives as selling their homes or refinancing in the form of reverse mortgages.

"People don't bat an eye at borrowing for vacations, for a house or for a fridge, stove or furniture," Charlton says. "Canadians have taken on billions of dollars in credit card debt. They should open their eyes and see how borrowing can help secure their financial future."

There. I couldn't have said it better myself. (In fact, I did. Thank you, Ms. Hemeon.)

So, there you have them — the Five Laws to Create Wealth. I believe in them so passionately, I want to repeat them all here:

1. Pay yourself first.
2. Set articulated financial goals.
3. Be a contrarian: ignore the stock market and take the road less travelled.
4. Leverage human resources.
5. Leverage capital, by borrowing to invest.

I can think of no better way for people to guarantee that they will be able to smile happily and securely when they are confronted by the 65- or 70-year-old person who dwells within themselves.

So much for rules. What of the Amazing Three Ts?

10

The Simple Equation of Wealth Creation: The Amazing Ts

E VERY schoolchild has heard of — but hardly understands! — Albert Einstein's famous equation of $E = mc^2$ (energy equals mass multiplied by the speed of light squared).

However, few people know, and most certainly do not understand, the following equation, which will never win me any Nobel Prize but is guaranteed to make every reader of this book a lot of money over the next few decades, if they only heed it:

$$WC = T + T + T$$

Before you break into the same sweat that you did when confronting chemistry exams back in high school, let me quickly translate this for you:

Wealth creation equals the three Ts, or benefits, of compounding: Time, Total rate of return, and Taxation.

Now, what do I mean by each of these precious, wealth-creating Ts?

The Power of the First "T": Time

The best way I can capture the incredible power and glory of compound interest in creating wealth is by recalling one of the great myths of the American people: the sale of the island of Manhattan by the native people who lived there in the early seventeenth century for (purportedly) $24 worth of trinkets.

Whether or not this actually happened, let's use this seemingly bad real-estate deal to illustrate my point. Had these native Americans taken that money offered to them by the Dutch settlers in cash, and invested it at 8% annually at a bank, that $24 would be worth today — around 370 years later — a total of $50 trillion. You read right: *$50 trillion.*

To put that amount in a bit of perspective, let us note that the national debt of the United States today is around $3 trillion. And the total amount of publicly-traded securities on all the stock market exchanges of the United States is only around $1.5 trillion.

So, with the $50 trillion earned from that original $24, the descendants of the those early real-estate-selling native Americans could purchase the entire country, and not just the island of Manhattan, many times over.

Obviously, three-plus centuries is a long period of time, but the point is still relevant: interest compounded year after year after year can lead to some pretty astonishing amounts, if left alone. The benefits of compounding can be truly amazing, *when they are given time to work.*

The Power of the Second "T": Total Rate of Return

When we wish to look at the second of our three Ts, all of them necessary for wealth creation, let's continue our analogy of the native Americans who sold Manhattan for so very little money.

Let us say that those Indians could not find a bank that would provide them with 8% annual interest, and they had to settle for only 6% on their $24 investment back in 1626. You may be stunned to discover that, over the same period of 370 years, when that tiny amount was invested at 6% compounded annually, their descendants would now discover that their great inheritance was $50 *billion*.

Now, $50 billion is not a paltry sum, but please realize my key point here: by investing at a rate of only 2% less than they had hoped — 6% compounded annually, rather than the first example of 8% compounded annually, our Indian friends would eventually end up with only *one thousandth* of the value from our first example!

Think about it: $50 trillion, down to $50 billion because of a lousy 2% lower interest rate. What better example of the power of total rate of return could we possibly have than that?

The Power of the Third "T": Taxation

When we look at taxation — that inescapable and always important part of life and, yes, of wealth creation — we shall leave our billionaire (or, if even luckier, trillionaire) native Americans for a while and turn to our own selves, today.

As I have declared elsewhere in this book, Revenue Canada (or the Internal Revenue Service in the United States) is our partner in all of our investments. The question should be, how can we lessen *their* percentage of involvement in this unwilling partnership, and in a totally legal, acceptable fashion?

All investors are concerned about the capital gains tax, which we are all hit with when we list various "gains" (from stocks, bonds, mutual funds, GICs, Canadian or U.S. Savings Bonds, etc.) in our annual income tax return. But — and this is crucial — capital gains tax does not exist if you are a long-term buy-and-hold investor! Taxes are accruing, of course, but *no* taxes need be paid until you choose to sell!

Conventional wisdom declares that "no one has ever gone broke taking a profit." I do not think that way. Why? Because there are huge advantages for an individual who chooses to get into a position where he or she makes but a few superior investments, and then just sits back and watches them grow (over time, our first T, and with an ever-growing total rate of return, our second T), just like those very wealthy descendants of the Manhattan-dumping native Americans in our earlier example. The advantages of buying and holding are endless:

- You will pay a lot fewer brokerage fees when you buy and hold.
- You will pay far fewer taxes to the government when you buy and hold.
- You can legally and happily delay paying any capital gains taxes indefinitely through this wise strategy of not selling your investments continually.

- Through proper estate planning, your heirs will be able to inherit your estate with as little taxation as possible on what you leave them.

To powerfully dramatize the benefits of that third T — taxation that is wisely deferred — imagine that you could invest one dollar every single year for 20 years, and have it *double over each of those years*. (I must thank Robert Hagstrom for this inspired example.)

If you were in a 34% tax bracket, and you chose to sell your investment at the end of the first year, you would pay 34 cents in taxes on that one-dollar profit you made.

Now, of course, you are left with only $1.66 of your $2.00, to be reinvested, once again, at that attractive 100% annual return we discussed.

If you repeated this action every year for those two decades — sell your profit, pay the full capital gains tax, and then continue to reinvest the rest at that wonderful rate of 100% — you would have a gain of $25,200 at the end of the twentieth year, after paying taxes of $13,000.

If, on the other hand, you purchased that same one-dollar investment that doubled each year, and chose not to sell it until the end of the twentieth year, you would achieve a gain of $692,000, after paying taxes of approximately $356,000.

Therein lies the power of the third T — taxation. By buying and holding, both you and the government of Canada have profited far more — no, wildly more — than if you had sold and bought every year over the two decades.

So What's That Formula Again?

It's a lot easier than Einstein's, and a lot more fun for both you (in your retirement) and your children and grandchildren (when you leave them a very, very generous inheritance). The astonishingly simple formula is worth repeating here:

$$WC = T + T + T$$

In other words, Wealth Creation equals (maximum) Time, plus (maximum) Total Return, plus (minimum) Taxation.

As you may have surmised by now, everything that I have been sharing with you to this point in this chapter — from the wealthy native Indians to the wealthy buy-and-holder who wisely avoids wasting his fortune in regular capital gains taxes — fits in perfectly with the (similarly simple) theories of my mentor Warren Buffett.

Which is why we now go . . .

Back to Buffett

You recall from the earlier chapters and my Five Laws of Wealth that we have just completed listing that multibillion-aire investor Warren Buffett not only invested in many publicly-traded securities but he also invested in several businesses of which he owned 100% of their stock.

Indeed, over the past three decades, Mr. Buffett would often speak of his many investments in his wise and witty annual reports of his holding company, Berkshire Hathaway, and how interesting it is that he never differentiated his passion for one (the ownership of minority interests in some companies) over the other (his 100% ownership of several other firms). To quote from his 1993 annual report, "An investor who owns a small piece of an outstanding business should hang on to it with the same tenacity as an individual who owned 100% of a company."

Walking his talk over the past year, Mr. Buffett purchased the remaining 49% of GEICO, the giant insurance company of which he had held 51% for so many years, and actually invested $1.5 billion in September 1996 to purchase all the shares of a major flight simulator company — generously adding each to the worth and value of every share of Berkshire Hathaway stock.

Let's not miss the major point I'm making with the above paragraph: Warren Buffett has not only held on to chunks of major companies (Coke, Gillette, Washington Post, World Book, several fine shoe companies, etc.) for many decades, and never sold them, but he has actually avoided paying dividends to his many (happy) shareholders!

That may shock the majority of my readers. "But I have always been told to purchase stocks that pay dividends!" you might say. "Don't the best stocks give out dividends when they have good years?" each reader may well exclaim.

But don't you see? By not paying out many millions of dollars of dividends to the shareholders of Berkshire Hathaway, and by ploughing back into his company all those tens of millions of dollars in dividends that his firm had been receiving (from Coke, Gillette, etc.) over the years, Mr. Buffett was able to — much like those lucky Indians whose ancestors had invested their $24 and never touched the compounded interest — build up *massive* amounts of money! And with that money, he was able to simply reach into the pot and purchase the remaining shares of GEICO and that huge flight simulator company!

Warren Buffett would never have been able to buy those firms had he been paying out endless dividends to his shareholders. He simply kept reinvesting those dividends into his dozens of major companies, like our wise billionaire/trillionaire Indian ancestors!

The Foolishness of Jumping In and Out of the Stock Market

The vast majority of the public, and — unfortunately — of brokers and mutual fund managers are continually preoccupied with the "lofty levels of the market," and, as a tragic result, are continuously trading in and out of the stock market, trying to achieve short-term gains.

This is one of the many investment "strategies" that involve forecasting and guesswork, and they are notoriously unreliable. I don't have to look very far to prove my point, and with great emphasis, too.

Across the top of the Report on Business section of the *Globe and Mail* on Tuesday, November 12, 1996, we encountered the following headline: "Funds Miss the Boat on Banks." The subheading of that (devastating, embarrassing) article explained their foolishness in greater detail: "Managers Didn't Own Enough of Hot Sector to Cash In on Surge in Prices."

What happened was this: Canadian bank stocks are hot. So hot, in fact, that even American investors and fund managers have been buying in like crazy, right through 1996. The reasons why they are so hot is obvious: interest rates are down; people are eager to borrow more than ever before; mortgages are being taken out on homes in record numbers; profits from credit card debts have skyrocketed (after all, there's lots of money to be made when you charge from 15% to 19% on people's credit cards while you're borrowing from the federal bank for only 4% or 5%!). For over a year now, each of Canada's major banks has been announcing record profits — that's profits, not earnings — of a billion dollars and even more, every single quarter!

It seems pretty obvious that bank stocks would soar, doesn't it?

And they have. The stock prices of Bank of Montreal, the Royal, Toronto Dominion, and the others actually shot up over 30% — nearly a one-third increase in value — between August 31 of 1996 to a few days before the publication of that *Globe and Mail* article, in mid-November of the same year.

Yet what did the geniuses at the various mutual funds — the so-called managers of your billions of dollars of investments, RRSPs, savings, etc. — decide to do? Why, they actually ignored these astonishing gains and chose not to purchase bank stocks for their mutual fund portfolios!

I found it interesting that one of the most successful mutual fund managers of the past several years was forced to mail out a newsletter to his tens of thousands of clients in which he admitted that he was "surprised by the strength of the financial services sector."

He was "surprised"! *Mortified* would be a better choice of words. Here is what the same gentleman declared in an interview with the *Globe and Mail* investment reporter Andrew Bell when asked if he owned many bank stocks:

"Nothing to speak of . . . We just missed them. Can't catch them all."

One wonders if some mutual funds "experts" could catch cold in a hospital influenza ward!

Here are some numbers to ponder, by both market "experts" and ourselves:

Between August 31, 1996, and November 8, 1996, financial stocks zoomed up over *30%*, as noted above.

Between those same 10 brief weeks (!), the entire Toronto Stock Exchange Index, which is made up of 300 stocks, shot up *12%* (since banks and utilities account for nearly 17% of that indicator). (A bit better than your GIC or CSB has been earning annually, yes?)

The shares of utilities were up *over 15%* during that minuscule period.

BCE Inc. of Montreal, once known as Bell Canada, leapt up *19%*.

Yet during those same few weeks (less than one-fifth of a year!), here is how some of the most popular mutual funds did — because they ignored bank and utility stocks:

C.I. Canadian Growth Fund increased 5.7%. (Not bad, for only a few weeks. But still . . .)

Industrial Growth Fund and Industrial Horizon Fund both gained the same amount as each other: 6.6%.

Altamira Equity Fund, one of the most successful mutual funds of the past decade, rose 3.4%. (Oh, yes. That often-impressive fund actually fell 1.54% in September, before gaining that 3.4% in October and early November.)

Do you remember what I've said about fear in this book? Read this comment from a prominent money manager as he explained why he wasn't buying bank stocks for his clients:

"I'm nervous about the banks when you've got interest rates 2% lower than U.S. rates. That's artificial. That can't be sustained for a long period of time."

I'm so sorry that this gentleman was nervous about purchasing bank stocks, especially when they've been announcing record earnings for over a year. But I'm more sorry for his hundreds of thousands of clients, who lost out on far greater returns than they received — all because of this (usually) brilliant man's fear.

Guess who *didn't* miss that dramatic run-up in the share prices of Canada's major banks in the fall of 1996? Investment managers such as Mike Lee-Chin of AIC Limited, who is a buy-and-hold man in the great Buffett tradition. In the mind of Mike, he is a "permanent shareholder" of the Bank of Montreal and the CIBC. Indeed, this same man, through the AIC Advantage Fund, has owned a large number of shares of a company called Fairfax Financial since the early 1980s. He purchased those shares at approximately $9 each. Today, including all the stock-splits and the reinvested dividends (remember my argument about not taking out dividends and having them taxed as capital gains, but rather leaving them in your portfolio!), each of those shares is valued, as of mid-1997, at around *$395!*

Now, imagine if Mr. Lee-Chin followed in the grand tradition of so many of the managers of great Canadian mutual funds who did not happen to have much faith in the financial sector of Canadian stocks in 1996. Would the extraordinary success story that is Fairfax Financial still be held tightly and closely in the AIC Advantage Fund portfolio today? I highly doubt it.

Businesses — like Diamonds — Are Truly Forever

As I note so often throughout this book, the root of all wealth creation lies in business ownership. In every country of the world, the richest people are those who own businesses. (Once again, by "owning a business," I mean not only complete ownership but also possessing common stocks of that business; do recall how Warren Buffett makes no differentiation between the way he treats his "ownership" of less than one-tenth of the shares of Coca-Cola and the 100% he now owns of GEICO and several shoe and furniture companies. He loves and respects each company equally, and enjoys the great profits of each by never touching their dividends, nor by buying and selling either's shares in a frivolous or panicky manner.)

But while the great value of business ownership may seem obvious, there is something that is too often *less* obvious: what I call the real value of a business, and sometimes its most important attribute. Surprisingly, this is overlooked by most people.

I suggest to you that *the most important* aspect of a business is its long-term ability to compound its earnings inside a "tax shelter" — in other words, the Three Ts that I discussed earlier. This is the astounding function of earnings, over time, without the negative effects of taxation.

This is a good place to give you a further example from the great Coca-Cola company. When that remarkable business first went public on the New York Stock Exchange in 1919, it cost a heady $40 a share. Sun Trust Bank of Atlanta was actually offered $100,000 in cash, in lieu of their underwriting fee, to get it on the exchange — or, if they preferred, they could be paid with a number of shares in the young company.

How wise they were to take the shares. Today, the common stock that Sun Trust chose to receive is valued *in excess of $2.5 billion!* And this valuation is not because some manic-depressive stock market had artificially elevated those shares up to insane, lunatic levels. This skyrocketing value in Coca-Cola shares was simply the result of that company's ability to compound its value (like our mythical investing native Americans at the start of this chapter).

Warren Buffett once made a rather surprising declaration: "There is little difference between a business and a bond!" How is that possible, you ask? Well, a bond will pay a fixed amount at a fixed rate for a certain period of time, correct? And a good business will do the same.

But here is a very attractive difference between the two: both bonds and businesses give income, but bonds have a fixed life span. Businesses can go on forever, and while their income can vary greatly (unlike a bond), they also have the potential of earning far greater percentages. And, best of all, a great and highly successful business can last for several generations, even indefinitely. Name a bond that can do that for you.

The great thing about both businesses and bonds is that magical Rule of 72, which many of you have read about, and which has actually been maligned as "the work of the devil," because it creates so much money with so little work. It's quite a lovely rule, which says simply that the length of time it takes for any investment to double in value is related to the number 72.

So, for example . . .

- If the rate of compound interest available from a business or a bond is 12%, it will take six years for the principal to double in value (i.e., good old 72 divided by 12 is 6).
- If you are getting 9% on your investment, it will take eight years for it to double in value.
- If you are getting 8% in interest, it will take nine years for your initial sum to double, and so on.

There is the thrill of compound interest in action. Which is why the Three Ts of Time, Total Return, and Taxation are so crucial to creating wealth. And by taking his Time, continually reinvesting his Total Return, and by not taking any money out, thus leaving it open to Taxation, Warren Buffett was able to turn a company worth a few hundred thousand dollars into a multibillion-dollar holding company in less than three decades.

(I should note that many of my own clients, when they hear me follow this line of reasoning, get extremely agitated: "What do you *mean* I should never sell? How can I enjoy my wealth? I don't want to leave *everything* to the kids! I want to live a little, too!" The answer I give them is quite simple: Systematic Withdrawal Plans, which shall be discussed in chapter 13.)

Where Most Investors — Including Mutual Fund Managers — Go So Horribly Wrong

I could spend this entire book describing the poor decisions of so many financial planners and even mutual funds managers, but I'll just list a few here, and note why they fail in their goal of creating wealth.

Sector Rotation Is Spinning Your Wheels

This concept is self-explanatory, really: The portfolio manager — whether the individual client or the man or woman who handles the purchases of a mutual fund — is always moving money around, as he or she sees fit. The favourite line of these people is "Buy low, sell high!" This so-called strategy is closely linked with "market timing."

I personally feel that this is the most stupid of all investment strategies, because common sense tells us that *it is utterly impossible to predict anything*! I have always found it informative that there is not one single wealthy individual listed on the famous Forbes Four Hundred (of the richest people in the United States) who is a market timer.

Even more important is the fact that sector rotation/market timing is terribly antagonistic to the Three Ts, since the frequent buying/selling violates the precious Time component, and, because of the occasional capital gains achieved, it violates the crucial Taxation component as well. Why give governments more than they deserve?

One of my favourite stories has to do with AIC Advantage Fund's purchase of large chunks of Trimark Financial stock at $12⅛. Now, since Trimark first hit the market at $12 even, back in 1992, what does that say?

I'll tell you what it says: That an awful lot of "investors" — bad gamblers, I'd prefer to call them — actually were satisfied enough with their giant one-eighth-of-a-dollar gain on their shares of Trimark (that's less than 13 cents, please note!) that they were eager to cut bait and take their "profit" after only a few hours of holding their stock!

And, as I note frequently in this book, each original $12

share of Trimark Financial is worth today — as of mid-1997 — over $280! But I guess that 13 cents was enough to make thousands of men and women happy. I hope they all proudly listed that impressive profit under capital gains in their 1992 income tax forms.

Asset Allocation Is No Better!

Asset allocation is simply a fancy way of saying "I'd better put my eggs — i.e., my savings — into as many baskets as possible, because I possess no conviction or belief whatsoever."

Why on earth should people buy a dozen different kinds of mutual funds — one handling bonds, one that invests in Japan, another that looks at "small cap" companies, one dealing in oil and gas, another in American equities, etc., etc., etc.?

Asset allocation may seem like an inspired way to cover all bases and to protect oneself. But as far as this writer is concerned, all it *mainly* protects is the investor from averaging more than mediocre returns each year. This kind of dubious strategy can easily violate all three Ts — Time, Total Rate of Return, and Taxation.

Thematic Investing Is No Better, Either

Themes are lovely in a symphony and in a literary novel, but I see no great glory in so-called thematic investing. Indeed, by choosing only oil-and-gas or gold, or small businesses, or whatever, you are, once again, *avoiding* the tremendous gains that are available from quality businesses in every field. And what of the Three Ts?

Momentum Playing — but Who Is Gaining Momentum?

Momentum playing in the stock market, which I like to call "The Greater Fool Theory," is equally flawed as a kind of investment strategy. Following this concept, a person buys stocks when they are "gaining momentum," and then sells them to someone else at a still *higher* price! Here, too, a person is ignoring the precious, invaluable equation of the Three Ts. Where, in momentum playing, do you see a person holding a stock (e.g., a business) for any length of time, or for long enough to achieve a good total rate of return, or in order to avoid excessive and unnecessary annual taxation?

Please remember our billionaire/trillionaire Indians, who invested the $24 that they foolishly accepted for Manhattan. Their descendants today could buy all of America several times over because of the magnificence of compound interest — the *true* value behind the great theory of the Three Ts.

Is compound interest really such a complex theory? Is the Rule of 72 actually as difficult to understand as Einstein's theory of relativity? I don't think so. And to prove my point, let me refer to a glorious human being who was utterly unknown before the summer of 1995. It was then that this now 88-year-old African-American woman, Oseola McCarty, chose to donate nearly her entire savings — $150,000 — to pay for scholarships to the nearby University of Southern Mississippi.

You may well have heard of this woman over the past year or so. After all, she was quickly written up on the front page of the *New York Times*, appeared on *Good Morning America*, was named one of the "10 Most Interesting People of 1995" by Barbara Walters, and much more. Why, the great jazz singer Roberta Flack sang to her, as did Patti LaBelle. President Clinton eagerly had his photo taken with her. Harvard gave her an honorary degree. Thousands of people have made pilgrimages to her tiny house in Hattiesburg, where she has lived all of her life, a home bequeathed to her a half-century ago by an uncle.

Now, why has the world been so taken by this quiet, shy, modest and deeply religious woman, who dropped out of school when she was only eight years of age, when she began to work as a laundress? Is it because she was so shockingly generous? (After all, Bill Gates of Microsoft, worth over $15 billion and annually in competition with Warren Buffett of Berkshire Hathaway as the World's Richest Man, gives away a few million dollars every month or so, and no one finds that particularly impressive.) Is it because this grade-school drop-out, never-married woman had — to quote the *New York Times* on November 12, 1996 — "spent very little over the years, living so simply, amassing a small fortune a few one-dollar bills at a time"?

I sense it was the latter that truly shocks us, and that's a shame. The sight of an elderly black woman giving away nearly every penny she ever earned to offer scholarships to a southern American university is what should *really* move people.

No, I think Ms. McCarty shakes people up for the wrong reason — she saved so much money with so little investing! And I found it touching that there is a new book coming out, titled *Simple Wisdom for Rich Living*, filled with this old woman's down-home opinions on faith, work, clean living, and saving money.

I was struck by the brief entry on the page on "savings":

"The secret to building a fortune is compounding interest."

So speaks Oseola McCarty, who managed to save $150,000 over her lifetime, a dollar at a time, while doing other people's laundry. Ms. McCarty is a grand soul, and she ultimately knows more about financial planning than many of the millionaire, so-called gurus of the stock market whom we've been reading about for decades.

She understands the power of compounding interest over time — so that taxation would not eat up her earnings — which allowed her to create college scholarships for generations to come.

The Three Ts work every time — and you don't need a Harvard MBA to understand the overwhelming power they possess. Just think of Miss Oseola McCarty of Hattiesburg, Mississippi.

(But should your tastes run to the more educated, might I conclude with a remarkable statement made by the great scientist Albert Einstein when he was asked if the recently exploded atomic bomb, which grew out of his theories of energy and physics, had "just unleashed the most powerful force in the world." "No," the genius replied, "the most powerful force is compound interest.")

11

Why Long-Term
Investments Are Best

THERE was a very funny cartoon carried in thousands of newspapers several years ago — it was from "Mother Goose and Grimm," as I recall — and it struck me as a very fitting way to begin this passionately felt, cry-from-the-heart chapter.

In that daily strip, Mother Goose has taken her cat to the vet. "Fetch!" the veterinarian yells at the cat.

The cat sits there.

"Jump!" the vet shouts.

The cat sits there.

"Roll over!" the vet orders.

The cat sits there.

The veterinarian turns to its owner and exclaims, "Your cat seems *perfectly* normal to me!"

The analogy quickly becomes clear: when your buddies, or your neighbours, or the business journalists, or even your broker all scream at you "Sell!" (because of real or imagined problems in the stock market, panic, fears, or even a mini-crash), simply respond like that wise, healthy, and "perfectly normal" cat of Mother Goose. Just sit tight and wait it out. Because you will *always* come out on top, as I'll prove to you now, with facts and statistics galore.

(One could even play on the word "dog" here, since that's a word often used for a stock that goes down steadily: For it is dogs, not cats, that are often eager to fetch, jump, and roll over — not cats, which are not about to move for *anyone*. When one is truly invested in the stock market — and not merely gambling, by leaping in and out of one's portfolio — then one must be clever, even lazy, like the wily cat, not the eager-to-leap-at-your-bidding dog. Cats simply have no interest in listening to their owners; they just love to lie around and sleep away their lives. Which is what your excellent portfolio of fine "businesses" should be doing — for year after year after year.)

As I write this book in mid-1997, the New York Stock Exchange has shot past the 7,600 mark on the Dow Jones, followed closely by Canada's own Toronto Stock Exchange as it moves well beyond 6,400. Naturally, this has a lot of people "worried" and "frightened" — and you already know my opinion about fear: what you fear the most will come upon you. Fear poverty, and you will surely be visited by it.

What are some of these fears, expressed almost daily by brokers, journalists, and analysts alike (and for the past several years in a row, by the way, as the stock markets of North America keep going up and up and up)?

- Dividends are too low!

- Stock prices are far too high!
- The mutual funds are buying too much, forcing those stock prices up artificially, and dangerously!

You may recall that I earlier described newspapers as "the Antichrist" of sensible investing. An example of what I spoke about blared out at me from a *USA Today* box in downtown Toronto. It was the Tuesday, November 26, 1996, issue, and here are just a few "gems" I plucked from its cover story entitled "Dauntless Dow: Too Far, Too Fast?"

> With the Dow Jones industrials setting *record after record*, posting a 28% gain this year on top of 1995's 33% gain, the notion of *perpetually rising prices* does not seem *outrageous*.
>
> . . . As recently as Oct. 11, the Dow had never closed above 6,000. In November, the average has climbed 8.6%. That's the biggest monthly rise since December 1991 . . .
>
> But *instead of celebrating*, professional money managers on Wall Street are *worrying* because the market has been making people so much money so fast.
>
> If things don't cool off soon, the amazing stock boom could be followed by a *sudden and dramatic bust or a painfully long bear market* . . .
>
> So good is the environment for stocks, that some are likening it to nirvana. And there is talk that the stock market has entered a new age where century-old measures of value are no longer relevant.
>
> All this *scares* market veterans. They know markets move from *one extreme to another*. The moves start with good reasons, but end after *too much fear*, or *too much*

greed. They know that in bull markets investors move from using reason to conjuring up rationalizations for *speculation.* (Emphasis added)

Are these doom-sayers right in their doom-saying?

They will certainly be (eventually) correct in one sense: there *will* be a correction in the stock markets of this continent, and probably around the world, over the next month/year/years — and I am writing this in June 1997.

How do I know? Because history tells me so. There are clear patterns in the behaviour of stock markets, just as there are in life. If you tell me that it has snowed in your city before December first every other year for a century, I think it's a pretty fair assumption that the chances are good that it'll snow before that date this year — or next. And if you've suffered from hay fever nearly every summer since you were a teenager, the chances are good that . . . (you see what I'm getting at).

Here's a fact for you — and I hope you won't let it fill you with fear: since 1900, stocks on the New York Stock Exchange have *declined* by at least 10%, and sometimes more than that, *on over 50 separate occasions.* That's an average of slightly more than one "major correction" every two years or so throughout this century.

Here's another fact: on fully 15 of those 50-plus corrections in the marketplace, stocks have gone down *fully one-quarter* of their price, or even more.

To put this another way, approximately every half-dozen years, the stock exchanges of North America experience some severe — if rarely long-lasting — setbacks.

Now, how should one react to these relatively frequent, if

unpleasant, occurrences in the stock market? Most people, sadly, tend to respond to any so-called bear market with panic selling, loss of faith in the stocks they were holding, disappointment with their broker, fears for their financial future. Yet the patterns of stock market corrections are there, and should surprise nobody.

As a parent, I cannot resist an analogy: If we screamed "I give up!" and threw our children bodily out of the house every time they talked back to us, disobeyed us, broke curfew, smoked behind our backs, or skipped school, our streets would be so filled with homeless youth, we wouldn't be able to move from store to store.

Yet that is precisely how the majority of "investors" act when the stock markets go through those periodic, almost regular, corrections! "Sell everything!" we scream at our broker. "I've had it with gambling! And I'm firing you, too!"

Stop Speculating — and Really, Truly Invest

Well, *I've* had it with speculating, too! Which is why I purchase only quality companies for my clients — since I recognize that in every correction, all companies (whether they are good, bad, or indifferent) see their stock prices decline. Recall that major correction in the last decade that I mentioned earlier in this book, the one that pushed Warren Buffett's amazing Berkshire Hathaway holding company down from $8,900 a share to less than $6,000. That's a brutal drop. But it didn't take long for wise investors to recognize that Berkshire continued to hold billions of dollars in Coke, Gillette, and dozens of other great businesses and had lost none of its inherent value. So what happened? Its stock price quickly rose far beyond its earlier high, to well over $47,600 in mid-June. Now *that's* a correction that most of us would welcome!

Yet these nearly inevitable corrections continue to freak out, depress, and terrify investors, *every single time*! And people respond by doing absolutely destructive things to their portfolios. They hedge their bets (as if long-term investing in solid businesses can ever be labelled "betting"!) by playing far more risky games on the market, such as "shorting" stocks (selling shares before you actually own them, while hoping that they will fall in value before you have to pay up). Or they buy options or futures, which I refuse to even discuss in this book. *It's all speculative behaviour!*

The other foolish thing that far too many "investors" do when these corrections occur is sell off large amounts of various stocks and mutual funds, and then sit on their diminished money, hoping that prices will fall lower and lower — but (naturally) they are never quite sure *when* they should climb back in.

And who can be sure? (You've already read my mockery of so-called market timing.) Indeed, most of the truly successful investors of our time, from John Templeton (founder of the Templeton mutual funds) to Peter Lynch (former fund manager at Fidelity Investments) to my own mentor Warren Buffett, are forever preaching how futile it is to attempt to guess which direction the markets are going to head.

I have noted throughout this book, and it's worth mentioning again, that corrections in the market are the *best* time to purchase quality firms at a good price!

I could give you ten thousand statistics of solid companies that have been battered during the several dozen corrections of the past century, and prove to you how they *always* come back stronger than ever, like a good prize-fighter who gets knocked down briefly and climbs up again. Here are simply a few — quite striking — examples of some great American stocks over the past quarter-century.

Banc One Corp. hit a low of $1.60 in 1974, after having reached $2.87 a share the year before. During that "crash" of 1987 that everyone still talks about with horror, its stock crumbled to $9.70 after peaking at $16.12 in the same year. As of late January 1997, as I wrote this book, one share of Banc One cost you over $43. In June 1997? $50.

Is that "recovery" enough for you? No? Then how about the common stock of Disney, which hit a low of 97 cents during the correction of 1973/74, after reaching a high of $6.89. During 1987, its stock fell from $20.63 to $10.31. Today, Disney shares go for close to $80 each.

Since most of us enjoy eating hamburgers almost as much as visiting Disney World, let's look at McDonald's shares over those same periods. In 1973/74, that great company's shares veered between $3.80 and $1.05; in 1987, the range was $15.28 and $7.84. Today? Over $48 a share.

Procter & Gamble is another company whose products we use frequently, even daily. How did its shares do in each of those periods? Back in the early 1970s, P&G common stock ranged between $8.38 and $15; in that scary "crash of '87," it slumped from a high of $42.44 to a low of $15. In late 1996, you had to pay over $107 for a single share; in mid-1997, over $139!

And we mustn't ignore those two favourite companies of Warren Buffett of Berkshire Hathaway, to whom I frequently refer and pay homage. Coca-Cola and Gillette both show similar successes, after similar roller-coaster rides. The soft-drink stock ranged between $1.86 and $6.25 in 1973/74; in 1987, between $7.00 and $13.28; and today, it's selling for over $71 a share — after a recent 2-for-1 split, of course.

And Gillette? The early 1970s saw it drop from $4.13 to $1.30; 1987 witnessed a crumbling from $11.47 down to $4.41. Today? Big surprise. In late November 1996, one share was worth over $81; in late June 1997, it was $96!

And you wondered why Warren Buffett is one of the wealthiest men in America? And maybe you still wonder, as well, why you — and millions of others — panic needlessly every time the stock markets of the world undergo those fairly regular "corrections." As Peter Lynch, the great investor, once noted about the chairman of Berkshire Hathaway's billion-dollar personal fortune: "He got there by picking stocks and not by switching in and out of them."

What's Gained — and Lost — by Jumping In and Out of the Market

Stocks — like sports teams and the careers of movie stars — have their good and bad years, and the stock markets of the world have good and bad months. Here are some choice comments from Peter Lynch, which I found in both speeches and in print over the past few years. They are well worth pondering.

> People who exit the stock market to avoid a decline are odds-on favorites to miss the next rally. If you don't believe corporate profits will continue to rise, and you can't stomach a decline in the market, don't buy stocks or equity mutual funds.

If you were out of stocks in 40 key months over the past 40 years, your annual return on investment dropped from 11.4% to 2.7%. You underperformed your savings account.

Since 1965, if you bought stocks once a year and were unlucky enough to pick the worst day to invest (when stocks were at their highest prices) 30 years in a row, you ended up with an annual return of 10.6%. If you were incredibly lucky and invested on the best day of the year 30 years in a row, you ended up with an annual return of 11.7%. So the difference between perfect timing and horrendous timing is 1.1%. This timing business is much ado about very little.

Stocks outperformed bonds in eight out of the nine previous decades in this century, and they are well ahead halfway through this one [the 1990s].

As Warren Buffett, Peter Lynch, and I would all put it: stick around, and don't bail out, when those relatively regular "corrections" happen. And if you do panic, remember Mr. Lynch's numbers, and some of the stock price swings of Disney, McDonald's, Coke, and Gillette, and dozens of other quality, innovative, ever-growing companies over the past quarter-century. Those numbers should certainly give you strength to carry on, and hold on — like the most successful investors do.

But Why "Risk" Playing the Stock Market at All?

The above is a perfectly legitimate question that many millions of North Americans ask themselves, and that, unfortunately, a good percentage of them choose to answer in the negative.

So what do they do instead? They play it safe, by tip-toe-ing gently into the very safe (and very predictable) (and *exceedingly unprofitable*) world of GICs, treasury bills, and bonds. The people who are most guilty of this are those who are retired, and/or over 65, and who fear that, with no more money coming in from their jobs, they'd better avoid "those dangerous up-and-down stocks."

Wrong, wrong, wrong. And to prove my point, I turn to a quite fascinating recent study by three finance professors at York University in Toronto, who put together a very impressive study that suggested that — and I here quote the *Globe and Mail* article on professors Kwok Ho, Moshe Arye Milevsky, and Chris Robinson — "holding substantial equi-ties [e.g., stocks] in retirement actually *increases* long-term safety." (Emphasis added)

In other words, seniors who buy and hold stocks not only will live in far better style in their later years but will actually minimize the horror of so many older people: that they might outlive their savings. (Such as what happened to that tragic couple in their 80s who came to my office in the fall of 1996, and whom I described earlier in this book, just before I listed the Five Laws to Create Wealth.)

What the professors discovered deserves stressing here: equity investments — i.e., stocks — out-perform fixed-income ones, such as GICs, CSBs, and U.S. Savings Bonds, by a wide margin!

Professor Robinson of York quotes from Statistics Canada mortality tables, and although they are very hopeful for those of us who wish to live long lives they can be extremely discomfiting for those of us who have not thoughtfully finan-cially planned for the future. A woman who has made it to the age of 65 today has a 50% chance of living to the age of 85, a 31% chance of making it to 90, and a 12% chance of living until the age of 95.

And what about today's 65-year-old man? He has a 28% chance of living to 85, a 15% chance of making it to 90, and a 4% chance of living until he is 95.

When the good professors of York University looked at those statistics, they concluded, "If you want to choose a planning horizon, it should be at least 95 for a woman and 90 for a man."

Now, that's all well and good, if you've got a million bucks socked away, and how many of us have been fortunate enough to achieve that?

But notice what these scholars discovered, using a relatively familiar situation.

A 65-year-old woman retires with $560,000 in savings, and wishes to have, say, $40,000 each year in inflation-indexed income. (This means that, because of inflation, the 40 grand she needed in the first year after leaving the workforce will turn into $42,000 in the second year, and then more and more and more as time goes on.)

Here's the horror story: that cautious 65-year-old woman who invested her money in, say, treasury bills will have a 65% chance of outliving her capital!

But if she took the same money and invested 95% of it (or more) into quality common stocks, that horrific probability of running out of money falls to *only 28%*.

Even the average man, with his traditionally shorter life span, encounters a similarly scary ride with those so-called safe and prudent investments. In the same situation, a 65-year-old man will still have a 45% probability of outliving his accumulated capital with all of his money in T-bills. Yet this probability falls to a mere 19% if he holds 90% or more of his savings in equities.

The way these three York professors reached the above conclusions is very interesting. They noted that in the 43 years between 1950 and 1993, the average annual (after-inflation) return on 91-day Canadian treasury bills was a mere 1.5%.

Government of Canada long-term bonds produced a return that was little better: a measly 2.8%.

Yet over the exact same period, the Toronto Stock Exchange 300 composite index returned an average of 7.7%. The man and woman I've been describing could have retired with millions if they had chosen to buy quality stocks in excellent businesses, whether in Canada or the United States, and would never even come close to finding them-selves outliving their capital.

The York University professors give many other examples in their study, but the point they make should already be both clear and vital. Even with those sometimes nerve-wracking fluctuations that I've been describing in this chapter as "corrections" (for T-bills, the variance has aver-aged a mere 3.9%; for bonds, 10.4%; for stocks, 17.2%), to quote Professor Robinson, "equities remain crucial, because of their higher long-term returns."

Which is why I continue to stress through this book: buy quality businesses, or parts of good businesses (as repre-sented by their common shares listed on public exchanges), and hold them for long lengths of time, while continually reinvesting any dividends. The result will invariably be a happy, worry-free retirement — unlike the sad stories of men and women who continually turn to GICs, treasury bills, and bonds. They — perhaps surprisingly to many a reader — are the true risk-takers in the world of investing, not those who choose to invest in good businesses. Cash was never intended to be a storehouse of value, and it should not be used that way.

The Israelis were once asked, after one of their many victories over far more numerous and well-armed enemies, why they kept winning, and they answered with an interesting expression: *Ayn B'rayra* — "There is no alternative." It was a powerful declaration: the Arabs can lose a battle and still have their countries, their leaders, their nations. If we Israelis lose even once, they explained, we would be doomed and have nothing to fall back on. With all due respect, I think the phrase "There *is* no alternative" could be applied to anyone who feels that they can rely upon GICs or Canada Savings Bonds for their future: There is no alternative to careful, thoughtful, wise, long-term investing.

As I said at the opening of this chapter, be a cat in the world of equities, and not a dog. Don't jump, fetch, or leap for anyone — even in response to the largest correction in the market. Just curl up and sleep — on a soft, warm, blanket of good common shares of excellent businesses, and quality mutual funds. And avoid the so-called safe world of GICs, treasury bills, and bonds as you would the plague.

12

Buy Mutuals — but Buy Their Stocks

AS a man who has made a fine living over the past two decades by recommending mutual funds to my clients, I am not about to bad-mouth that admirable investment vehicle. Indeed, since the fund that I co-founded back in the mid-1980s, AIC, has seen its Advantage mutual fund shoot up from an initial offering of $5 to over $62 at the time of my writing this book, I am well aware of just how wonderfully mutual funds can grow for their investors. *Especially* when they are run by people who firmly believe in the principles I've been stressing throughout this book. And which I am now doing, with the new family of Infinity mutual funds!

But I'm now about to make a declaration that may seem surprising to many, but it sure won't be so shocking once I give you the facts and figures. Here goes:

There is *no* mutual fund that can grow as rapidly or as successfully as a publicly-traded mutual fund company.

Think about this for a few moments, please.

Any mutual fund — no matter how excellent its managers, no matter how wise and thoughtful (and lucky) its owners — *must* invest in many different stocks and bonds. That is their mandate, and many do it with brilliance.

But think about the mutual fund industry, if you will. It is the joyful recipient of an astounding, astonishing boom, which goes back over a quarter-century. In 1977, exactly twenty years ago, the total amount of money invested in mutual funds across North America was approximately $50 billion, which seemed impressive at the time.

Today, that number is in excess of $3.7 *trillion*! Indeed, there are now more mutual funds available than there are stocks listed on the New York Stock Exchange!

Let's look at Canada alone: When I first joined the field in 1979, there was less than $1 billion invested by our fellow countrymen in mutual funds. Ten years later, it was perhaps $5 billion. Today, that sum is rapidly approaching $260 billion! And experts were predicting, in the first weeks of 1997, that close to $40 billion *more* would be invested in mutual funds by the end of that year's RRSP season, March 1!

The Times, They *Are Really* A-Changin'

Scholars like to describe poets and artists as the "antennae" of society, and in many ways they are. Oftentimes, great writers and artists suggest, even predict, massive changes about to affect society, long before economists, professors, politicians.

But the occasional businessman can also have very acute antennae himself. I think of Henry Ford, who was hardly the first person to "invent" the automobile, but he was, inarguably, the genius who created the assembly line, which eventually put North America, and the entire world, on wheels.

Ford did something else that was just as inspired: he offered "five dollars a day!" as wages in the early 1930s, at a time when the vast majority of other businesses were paying their employees only a dime, maybe a quarter, an hour. "He's crazy!" exclaimed most of America's politicians and economists. "He'll go broke!"

Henry Ford thought otherwise, and we know now who was correct. He had figured out that if he gave his employees large enough wages, they would be better able to purchase the automobiles they were assembling!

Ford was a visionary, and his antennae were certainly amazing. But I'm not sure how visionary anyone has to be to look around and see the massive changes that have been occurring for several decades in the saving and investing habits of North Americans.

I've suggested this, earlier in this book. We are going through one of the most powerful demographic shifts in history, across North America and around the world. As the tens of millions of so-called Baby Boomers edge into their 50s and prepare for their respective retirements, they are no longer convinced (as their parents had been) that their governments will have the ability (much less the philosophy or even desire) to fund their retirement and healthcare through social service programs and the so-called safety net.

One does not even have to read the daily paper to make note of the slashing away at various programs by Ottawa, and in more and more provinces, from Alberta to Ontario and beyond. Not only are there massive deficits on both federal and provincial levels, but the one or two retired people of today who have nearly a half-dozen other working Canadians paying into Canada Pension for them will soon change to a half-dozen people in retirement for every *one* person still on a payroll. Worker-to-retiree percentages are similarly scary in the United States as we move beyond the millennium.

Is it any wonder that mutual funds have become an attractive investment? And here is what is most relevant to this chapter, as well as to the theme of this book: mutual fund companies — several of which have publicly-traded stocks on exchanges around the world — fall into that same category I've been stressing throughout this text. They are superior businesses that are in strong, long-term growth industries. And if they are run with honest, careful share-holder-managers, they will create great value.

But here is where mutual fund stocks differ from, say, minor soft drink companies or merely competent computer businesses: even mediocre mutual fund company stocks are good investments, because of this extraordinary momentum, this hurricane-like wind in the sales of the mutual fund industry!

I wish I could claim some kind of epiphany, like Saul of Tarsus purportedly had on the road to Damascus in the Bible, where I suddenly "woke up" to the phenomenal potential — and actual growth! — in the stocks of mutual fund companies.

Alas, it was far less prosaic; indeed, it took several years to sink in. Here's what happened. Back in the 1981 recession, when I was in my third year of selling mutual funds, I found the resistance of buyers to be exceedingly high.

High? The CN Tower of Toronto and Chicago's Sears Tower would look like two-storey buildings in comparison. My good friend Michael Lee-Chin and I, as I noted back in chapter 1, had been selling mutual funds for one of the great mutual fund sales firms of Canada, Regal Capital Planners in the Hamilton, Ontario, area, and the winter was bleak. And I don't mean just the weather.

Interest rates were up to a usurious 21% — meaning that people were not too eager to invest in mutual funds — or anything else, for that matter. There was simply too much competition for their inflation-battered money.

Indeed, Canada Savings Bonds were offering a stunning 19% that same year, also putting the mutual fund industry in the shade, if not leaving it in the dust.

It was punishingly difficult to make any mutual fund sale! It got so bad, I was seriously considering a return to the insurance business, which I had left with some relief only a few years earlier. And Michael was even thinking of returning to his original home and native land of Jamaica.

Around this same time, Mackenzie — one of the largest mutual fund companies in Canada — decided to move from its humble beginnings over a fish-and-chips shop, with which it shared premises with one of its benefactors at Cara Foods. So Michael and I visited their snazzy new offices at 150 Bloor Street West in Toronto.

We were both dazzled by what we saw. Who can these people be? Beautiful china! Impressive hors d'oeuvres! Magnificent wood panelling! These people must have been *printing* money, while Michael and I were struggling to make ends meet!

In retrospect, they *were* printing money, and there was

good reason why we salesmen were not doing very well. We had the added burdens of maintaining staff, having client services in place, and encountering significant buyers' resistance to mutual fund sales. As Bob Dylan wittily sang, some years earlier, "Something is happening, and you don't know what it is — do you, Mr. Jones?"

We didn't know, even then. I'd just love to claim a sudden insight, like Henry Ford must have had with his five-dollar-a-day concept, or a religious epiphany like Saul-turned-Paul. But it took me and Michael another year or two, until it finally hit home: a mutual fund company is a fantastic, reliable, trustworthy investment!

My friend was struck by the potential of the common stock of Mackenzie Financial, which was then selling in the range of 50 to 60 cents on the Toronto Stock Exchange. So he went ahead and arranged a loan (remember my Fifth Rule of Wealth — *borrow to invest*) — and he invested heavily in the common shares of Mackenzie.

I almost hate to think about what his original investment is worth today, because knowing Michael Lee-Chin, whose philosophy is the same as mine and Warren Buffett's, he probably never sold it. Mackenzie common stock has gone from strength to strength to strength ever since, as you'll see below.

Another Writer's Thoughts about the Greatness of Mutual Fund Companies' Stocks

I've been confessing how slow I was to recognize the spectacular growth in the very industry in which I laboured. Thank heavens I wasn't alone in this blindness. (How many people saw the explosion in the number of cars on the streets and highways of North America back in the 1910s and 1920s, and promptly opened gas stations or tire companies or repair shops?)

Peter Lynch, labelled "the #1 money manager" by *Time* magazine, made a rather mortifying confession in his 1989 bestseller, *One Up on Wall Street*:

> Who could have had a greater advantage than yours truly, sitting in an office at Fidelity during the boom in financial services and in the mutual funds? . . .
>
> I'd been coming to work here for nearly two decades. I know half the officers in the major financial-service companies. I follow the daily ups and downs, and I could notice important trends months before the analysts on Wall Street. You couldn't have been more strategically placed to cash in on the bonanza of the early 1980s. [Author's note: The bonanza continues, a decade and a half later, and it will not stop for many years to come, if ever.]
>
> The people who print prospectuses must have seen it — they could hardly keep up with all the new shareholders in the mutual funds. The sales force must have seen it as they crisscrossed the country in their Winnebagos and returned with billions in new assets. The maintenance services must have seen the expansion in the offices at Federated, Franklin, Dreyfus, and Fidelity. The companies that sold mutual funds prospered as never before in their history. The mad rush was on.
>
> Fidelity isn't a public company, so you couldn't invest in the rush here. But what about Dreyfus? Want to see a chart that doesn't stop? The stock sold for 40 cents a share in 1977, then nearly $40 a share in 1986, a 100-

bagger in nine years, and much of that during a lousy stock market. Franklin was a 138-bagger, and Federated was up 50-fold before it was bought out by Aetna. I was right on top of all of them. I knew the Dreyfus story, the Franklin story, and the Federated story from beginning to end. Everything was right, earnings were up, the momentum was obvious . . .

How much did I make from all this? Zippo. I didn't buy a single share of any of the financial services companies: not Dreyfus, not Federated, not Franklin. I missed the whole deal and didn't realize it until it was too late . . . [Author's note: It's still not too late; see below.]

In his follow-up volume in 1993, *Beating the Street*, Peter Lynch admitted once again how he (seemingly, but not really) missed the boat on the explosive growth of mutual fund company stocks, and then added an interesting comment, well worth repeating here, because it emphasizes one of the major themes of my own book, which you are now reading: corrections, that is, those regular dips in the stock market, should be seen as fabulous opportunities to pick up stocks at bargain prices.

After noting the "fear of the collapse of the mutual-fund industry after the Great Correction of 1987," Lynch declares,

That correction gave me the chance to buy these fellow mutual-fund companies, which I had overlooked before, and at low prices. Here is another of my favorite what-if portfolios: If you had divided your money equally among these eight stocks [Dreyfus, Franklin Resources, Colonial Group, T. Rowe Price, State Street Bank, Alliance Capital

Management, and Eaton Vance] and held them from the beginning of 1988 to the end of 1989, you would have out-performed 99 percent of the funds that these companies promote.

Thinking about Peter Lynch and quoting from his two books makes me think of another major point I wish to make here. His boss at Fidelity, Ned Johnson, is among the top 10 richest people in America, because he owns 100% of that company. (He chose his father well, and inherited it; we should all have such problems.) As Lynch noted in his books, Fidelity is not public, so the only person who truly benefited from it is that one man, Ned Johnson, whose family firm manages over $500 billion in mutual funds today.

But isn't it informative that the brilliant, creative stock-wheeler-and-dealer Peter Lynch, who was Fidelity's most famous manager for many years, has never come close to being in the Forbes Four Hundred (richest people). Sure, he's worth tens of millions of dollars; he's invested well, and he's had two best-selling business books.

But Ned Johnson, his long-time boss at Fidelity, whom we hear of far less frequently than his most successful trader, is worth many billions of dollars — or over 1,000 times the for-tune of Peter Lynch!

You already know why Johnson is wealthier than Lynch; he owns a mutual fund company. And if *you* choose to (wisely) buy into a major mutual fund company's publicly-traded stock, *you* will own a mutual fund company too, just like Ned Johnson. Or at least a tiny piece of one. And, as noted above, mutual fund companies have the wind in their sails, and it will probably never stop blowing. After all, because of the shift from spending to saving amongst a growing number of aging Canadians, some predict that the mutual fund industry in Canada will have over *$1 trillion* invested in its products by the year 2005.

Why Mutual Fund Company Stocks Are the Way to Go

I've already suggested that there has been a tremendous demographic shift in North America, thanks to the tens and tens of millions of babies born when servicemen returned from the Second World War, who are now all edging into their 50s, and have money to invest in the "safety" and "security" of mutual funds.

But there is another reason why mutual fund companies are such fabulous investment possibilities. Let me make a few analogies to prove my point.

If you run a bakery or a fruit store, you've got to worry about your products going stale or rotten before you sell them. If you run a publishing company, you must be concerned with books that don't sell, advances-against-royalties that never get paid off, contracts that never get fulfilled, writers' blocks, lack of government grants, and more. If you run an oil company, you must worry about tensions in the Middle East, Arab boycotts, government taxation, reserves, etc., etc.

But if you run a mutual fund company — or own a common stock of one — you own a continuous revenue stream that flows from total assets under administration. No bread going stale or fruit going bad or books remaindered or oil shortages in the financial industry! No factories to heat, no tools to break down, no accounts receivable, no shipping,

no handling, no warehousing, no labor relations problems . . .
It is, quite literally, a perpetual money machine!

Here is something else that is quite interesting. Software
companies who do not market well or keep inventing new
and more creative products will go down the tube. The same
with dress shops or restaurants that don't keep up with fashion, or don't advertise well, or don't treat their customers
with respect.

Yet this is precisely where mutual fund companies also
differ, and substantially so, from nearly every other kind of
business or service industry. Even if a mutual fund practises
asset allocation (which I dislike), it will do well. Or uses sector rotation (which I consider foolhardy), it will grow. Or
leaps in and out of the market like a Mexican jumping bean
(which I abhor), it will succeed. Indeed, even if the money
manager of a mutual fund has his own twisted interpretation
of a "long-term-hold" on stocks as being "a maximum of two
weeks," it will thrive. Even if it holds cash for too long, or
emerging securities that never quite emerge enough, or buys
bonds — all of which I disdain — it will go from strength to
strength to strength.

Why? Because management fees are generated on a continuous basis for any fund management company! Because
every single mutual fund share sold — and there are billions
of them — brings a little more money into the firm that handles it! So, when you own shares of a mutual fund company,
your revenue continually streams in from every single
mutual fund they manage — no matter how questionably
they choose to manage it. Owning the mutual fund company
is where it's at, not the mutual fund!

The above is only partly true, of course. Mutual funds are

an essential part of every financial portfolio — and I don't mean asset allocation here. Mutual funds may rise less than mutual fund company stocks and other great growth industries, but they also fall less in those trying times of correction. So, for smoothing out the edges, I always recommend mutual funds — especially ones such as the new family of funds, Infinity, which I launched in early 1997 with David Singh, the president of Fortune Financial, all of which invest heavily the Warren Buffett way — in quality businesses and, yes, in mutual fund company shares.

Everything I am sharing with you here is public knowledge; it's all in the public domain. But let's talk international mutual fund companies for a moment. Peter Lynch referred to Dreyfus zooming up a hundred-fold in just a few years. But look at these others, from both the U.S. and around the world.

T. Rowe Price went public in 1980, when it was managing some $20 million in its mutual funds; today, it handles over $70 billion of other people's money. So what happened to its stock on the NYSE? It grew by *over 1,000%* over the past decade. (Does that company handle a mutual fund that has gone up by 200%, much less five times that? Of course not — which is the point of this chapter.)

Perpetual Asset Management of Great Britain went public much later. If you had invested $10,000 in 1991, its best-managed mutual fund would be worth just over $25,000. But the same money invested in Perpetual Asset Management common stock would be worth over $500,000!

How about EquitiLink in Australia? Their best, Growth Link Trust, as they call their mutual funds Down Under, would have taken your $10,000 and turned it into just under

$22,000 between 1991 and today, which sure isn't very dis-appointing. But if someone had invested the same 10 grand in the common stock of EquitiLink? It shot past $42,000 in the fall of 1996.

And what of Mercury Asset Management, a huge United Kingdom unit trust company? Ten thousand invested in 1991 in their best fund, Mercury General, grew to just over $16,000. Its not-so-common stock? Up to nearly $50,000.

But who has to go around the world, changing your Canadian dollars into American, or into British pounds and Australian bucks? Let's look at our own beloved country, in both the following chart and in the following words.

AGF Management Limited is a fine Canadian mutual funds company, and you certainly would have done well investing $10,000 in its AGF Canadian (mutual) Fund in 1984; it would break $27,000 by the fall of 1996. If you had put another $10,000 into its AGF Special Fund Ltd., another mutual fund, you'd have broken $41,000. But if you had invested the same amount in its publicly-traded manage-ment company, your nest egg would have hit *over $176,000* as of the early summer of 1996, and *over $300,000* as I write these words a year later.

How about $10,000 invested in Trimark's Canadian Fund mutual fund in 1992? It broke $17,000 in July 1996. The same amount in its Trimark Fund? Over $22,000. But if you had invested in Trimark's stock on the TSE — your investment would have been worth over *$86,000* — and more than dou-ble again by mid-1997.

And what of Mackenzie Financial Corporation, whose new offices had so wowed Michael Lee-Chin and me back in the early 1980s? Ten thousand invested in 1984 in their

Industrial Growth Fund would be worth over three times that a dozen years later, and nearly four times as much had it been invested in their Industrial American Fund over the same years. But $10,000 in Mackenzie Financial Corporation stock in 1984 was worth *over $130,000* as of the summer of 1996, and 150% more as of the summer of 1997. (I can hardly keep up with the constantly rising market, and a book has to go to press some time!)

Over my many years working with Michael Lee-Chin to build AIC into a real force and huge success in the mutual fund field since the mid-1980s, I have often been asked why its funds have done so spectacularly well. After all, many mutual funds are successful one year, but are below-par the next; only a few make it into the top 10 year after year after year.

Well, people like to say that ideas are a dime a dozen, but as far as I'm concerned, it's the man or woman who implements those ideas who has the real value. Indeed, he or she is priceless.

The visionary responsible for the amazing growth of the AIC Advantage Fund, Michael Lee-Chin, had seen this phenomenal opportunity in the mutual fund industry itself — at the same time that Peter Lynch, the "genius" of Fidelity, down on Wall Street, did not — and asked himself, "What *better* way can my clients participate in the growth of this wonderful industry than by owning shares of publicly-traded mutual fund companies?"

And so, Michael made sure that AIC Advantage Fund became a significant shareholder in Mackenzie's stock, and later, AGF's, and ultimately those of Trimark and Dundee and C.I. Fund Management and Investors Group.

It was an irresistible combination of two inspired concepts: buying excellent businesses and holding them "forever," alias "the Warren Buffett way," and recognizing that mutual fund companies are among the greatest money-manufacturers in human history.

I hope that I've clearly explained the theory — no, really a rule — that I proposed at the start of this chapter: mutual fund companies, through their publicly-traded common shares, are an essential part of any successful portfolio. Of course, people should *also* own individual mutual funds — I heartily recommend the new Infinity family, of which I am the Chief Portfolio Strategist — since they invariably help smooth out the bumps.

I cannot stress enough what a fantastic future lies in store for the mutual fund industry, and the stocks of the major mutual fund companies don't accurately track what's happening out there. Analysts like Mark Maxwell have pointed out how the world of mutual funds will grow at ever-increasing levels, relative to other industries, and for numerous reasons. As the Baby Boomers prepare for retirement. As their parents die off, leaving them their homes (which will often be sold, with much of their value reinvested into mutual funds). Then there is the money that the parents of the Boomers will leave them. Many estimate a *trillion-dollar inheritance*, and I have no doubt that much of that, too, will find its way into mutual funds.

There is still more. Interest rates hit 45-year lows in late 1996, which pretty well destroyed any last resistance to purchasing mutual funds, and to "borrowing to invest." (Quite the opposite of what Michael and I encountered with the 20%+ interest rates in Canada back in the early 1980s.)

And then there are what I call "the GIC Refugees," who

are marching into mutual fund salespeople's offices across North America as they find themselves with no alternative but to do what they should have been doing for the past 10, 20, even 30 years. They come out of desperation, and many see mutual funds as their salvation. And they are probably correct in that assumption.

The best kind of mutual funds gives their investors a broad cross-section of financial services companies (such as Mackenzie stock, AGF stock, Trimark stock, etc.), along with other businesses that, in many ways, behave similarly to the booming mutual funds industry: revenue-generating, revenue-stream businesses such as cable and telecommunications, for example.

So, the wise mutual fund investor gets a diverse portfolio of businesses in the best of the mutuals available today.

But without mutual fund companies' stocks in one's financial portfolio, one is truly missing the boat, like the often-brilliant Mr. Lynch admitted doing.

Oh, I should note one more thing: That boat is forever leaving the dock, yet it is *always* there for the boarding. Of course it is now too late to buy Trimark at its original $12, or even its present $180+ (when you figure in all the splits and dividends). But it will keep going up, not unlike Coke, Gillette, and other great businesses on the stock markets of the world. It's *never, ever too late* to buy into a quality company and own a share of Greatness.

Can you think of any reason why these financial institutions *won't* keep increasing in price and value? I certainly cannot.

Not with tens of millions of Baby Boomers waking up to their rapidly approaching retirements, governments cutting back on pensions and social programs, hundreds of billions of dollars of inheritances being left by parents for their children and grandchildren, and a world always thirsting for more soft drinks, more razor blades, more newspapers and magazines, more hamburgers, more insurance, more clothing — and, of course, more quality stocks and superior mutual funds.

13

Systematic
Withdrawal Plans

I have been stressing at great length, throughout this book, how crucial it is for every investor to buy and hold good, quality businesses (e.g., common stocks and/or mutual funds that hold the common stocks of those superior firms), yet I am often asked by my clients, "But how do I *live*? Where will I get the money for vacations, for that automobile that needs replacing, for my child's wedding (etc., etc.)? I can't simply sock away all of my savings into stocks and mutuals forever, even though you keep insisting that one should hold one's investments for that long!"

The answer is not only simple, but it is also remarkably money-saving — because it allows every one of us to legally keep our taxes low while maintaining the vast majority of our capital in those investments to continue growing and thriving!

The answer, as seen in the title of this chapter, is Systematic Withdrawal Plans, available from every broker and mutual fund dealer in Canada. Trimark, which runs some of the most successful and best-run mutual funds in the world, puts out a "taxation bulletin" that notes that "many Trimark unit holders have Systematic Withdrawal Plans that enable them to receive payments from their accounts on a monthly, quarterly or semi-annual basis." And so, they answer — in rather stiff and legalese language — the questions that are most frequently asked about the tax treatment of these plans. Here is a taste of what they have to say.

> Each systematic withdrawal is considered a redemption of units from a unit holder's account. A capital gain or loss is calculated as the difference between the total proceeds received (i.e., the systematic payments) and the average cost of the units redeemed. The average cost per unit at the time of redemption is the total cost at which all units were purchased before the redemption, divided by the total number of units outstanding at the time. An estimate of the realized capital gain or loss is provided to unit holders on a semi-annual basis on their account statements.

Are you lost yet? This is why taxation people should not write books! But the point that is being made here is essential, in spite of its dryness: when a person has a Systematic Withdrawal Plan — assuming, of course, that it is from a successful, decent portfolio, such as the mutual funds I shall be referring to below — they need not fear that they are depleting the capital of their investment.

This is crucially important, because it may come as a surprise to many readers. After all, if you pump water from a swimming pool, does it not eventually empty? If you take clothes from a closet, one by one, does it not eventually become empty?

The answer in the case of excellent mutual funds and stocks is a resounding no! for the simple reason that *while* you are slowly and regularly withdrawing funds from your portfolio (as opposed to that swimming pool or closet), the money that remains in those financial vehicles is continuing to grow.

And grow.

AND GROW.

The following few examples may astonish you; I certainly hope that they bring you pleasure — as they have for many tens of thousands of wise investors.

How a Systematic Withdrawal Plan Worked with the Trimark Fund over the Past 15 Years

Trimark began two mutual funds the same day — September 1, 1981. Let us say that you invested $100,000 at the very inception of the Trimark Fund, and have chosen to withdraw $825 every month, beginning 30 days after you invested $100,000; since the fund was "front-end load," your account value drops to $96,000 on the very first day, due to the 4% commission rate. But over the years, there would be capital gains distributions, changes (both up and down) in unit value, and more. Yet every reader of (and believer in) the principles expressed throughout this book would have *ignored* those daily fluctuations, and *ignored* the "scoreboard" (i.e., the mutual fund listings in the daily newspapers), and let that $100,000 investment grow and compound over those 15 years — while withdrawing that regular monthly amount of $825, of course.

Here are a few highlights from that experience to savour.

On December 31, 1983, after just over two years of withdrawing monthly, the value of your account was up to $155,387.

On December 31, 1988, five years later, your fund value had reached $218,228.

On December 31, 1993, five years after that — and after nearly a dozen years of withdrawing $9,900 every single year — the Trimark Fund Account had a value of $410,854.

And on June 30, 1996, your original $100,000 — in spite of your withdrawing over $140,000 over all those years, had magically turned into *$565,091*. (And far more, 12 months later.)

This is essential to emphasize here: in both of these cases, if you had put your $100,000 into a comparative plan that paid a fixed 10% return, you would have been able to withdraw those monthly amounts, of course, but you would have been left with $90,349 in your savings. That's right: your initial capital investment would have dropped nearly one-tenth over those same 15 years, instead of doubling, even quintupling.

What a difference!

How About if You Chose Templeton, Two Decades Earlier?

If the above numbers and descriptions of a successful Systematic Withdrawal Plan have not impressed you very much, let me truly blow you away with the following example of a very wise investor, who was fortunate enough to have $100,000 to spare back in 1964, and chose to invest in the Templeton Growth Fund, one of the great mutual funds of all time.

We will work this example almost the same way: You invest the sum, except on January 2, 1964, and begin withdrawing, monthly, the sum of $750 (or $9,000 annually) at once. In this case as well, all distributions of the fund will be reinvested, but we have chosen to index to inflation your withdrawals, so — for example — your $9,000 in your first year of withdrawal will reach $14,662 annually by 1975, $34,959 by 1985, and over $50,000 by 1995, in order to allow you to live in the way to which you are accustomed. Okay? Here goes. (Hold on tight!)

At the end of your first year in the Templeton Growth Fund, in which you withdrew that $9,000, the cash value in your fund had already hit $114,264, thanks to a rate of return of 28.40% that their brilliant managers had achieved over those initial 12 months.

Let's talk about a "bad year" for a moment, since I do *not* wish to leave readers with the belief that even the most superior mutual funds go up only in a straight line. Stock markets and stock prices go up and down; corrections are inevitable.

In 1970, during which time you withdrew $10,965 (since your monthly withdrawal is indexed to the inflation rate, as noted above), the rate of return of the Templeton Growth Fund was a *minus* 11.83%. Yet in spite of that, the cash value of your fund has now reached $141,665.

Jump to 1980: You withdraw $22,834 over that difficult year of runaway inflation (during which the Canadian Consumer Price Index shot up a whopping 11.2%), yet the cash value of your Templeton Growth Fund account is now an impressive $768,362. (Oh, yes — its rate of return hit 28.6% that year.)

One could do this for every year, but let's leap to 1994, when you withdraw an indexed-to-inflation $49,340 over those 12 months. The rate of return of the Templeton Growth Fund was only 3.8%, which must have been disappointing.

But you are not upset. You have withdrawn more than $770,000 over the 31 years since you first invested that $100,000 in 1964, which has allowed you to buy the occasional gift for a friend, and maybe a trinket or two for your spouse and children. And what is the cash value of your Templeton Growth Fund at the end of 1994?

Thanks to an average compound return of 17.09% over those three-plus decades, you now have a remaining cash value of $3,544,887. You read right: over $3.5 million in net asset value. (And much more, three years later!)

If you are as dazzled by these numbers as most of my clients have been, then let me frighten you a bit as well. For the smart men and women at Templeton also chose to set up a parallel situation: someone who invested $100,000 that same day in 1964, but into an investment "opportunity" that paid exactly 10% — indexed to inflation, of course, to be fair in the comparison.

Here's the horror part. That person who "avoided all risks" by sinking his or her $100,000 back in 1964 into that "safe" and "reliable" and guaranteed 10% investment vehicle — while withdrawing the same amount per month as our friend who "risked" investing in the Templeton Growth Fund — hit a peak cash value in his account of $103,546 in 1968, but then the account began to diminish by larger and larger amounts:

By 1973, the original $100,000 investment had dropped to

$98,081. By 1979, the capital had dwindled to $47,141. And by 1981, the original investment *had completely vanished*, and the "cash value" was in negative territory: minus $1,085.

That's right, good reader: the fear-of-risk investor had totally run out of money in less than a dozen years.

Want another scare? If that super-safe investor in the 10%-guaranteed vehicle *continued* to withdraw the same amounts as his friend invested in Templeton Growth Fund, by 1994 — when his dare-devil buddy now had a nest egg of over $3.5 million — he had an "overdraft" of $518,476.

So much for the safety of guaranteed vehicles, such as GICs, savings bonds, and the like. So much for them — and so little *from* them. (See chapter 14.)

Another major advantage of Systematic Withdrawal Plans is this: the money that you regularly take out from your financial portfolio is taxed at a much lower rate than pure capital gains; it's considered the return of your principal — part of your original investment. So you will be taxed by your partner at Revenue Canada or the Internal Revenue Service far less harshly than if you, say, bought and sold a stock for a quick killing and withdrew your profit at one fell swoop — or earned interest income from a GIC or bond, which is taxed 100%.

Just as buying and holding quality businesses (or superior mutual funds that buy and hold quality businesses) is the wisest way to invest, so Systematic Withdrawal Plans are the wisest way to redeem your ever-growing portfolio. Go over the examples I gave you from Trimark and Templeton mutual funds, above, and never forget this key thought: when you are redeeming a set amount every month of your mutual funds units, the remaining units over time will increase in value much faster than you are redeeming. In all my years of assisting my clients, we have never once exhausted a client's principal, because the pool never runs dry and the closet is never empty.

How Can I Save Taxes in Other Ways and Earn Income as Well?

In addition to Systematic Withdrawal Plans, investors should also look at vehicles such as Real Estate Income Trusts (REITs) and Royalty Trusts, which pay out tax-friendly income from real estate and oil and gas properties, respectively, as they generate profit.

Let's look at the former for a moment. Anyone who has even occasionally glanced at a newspaper over the past decade knows of the high flights and disastrous crashes of the real estate empires of those once-giants of Canadian Big Business, Robert Campeau and the Reichmann family (the latter with a private empire, Olympia & York). To this day, just hearing their names screams "Risk!" into investors' ears.

But the risk in real estate has always been in the leverage; that is, when people borrow huge sums of money in order to invest. Both Campeau and the Reichmanns lost their fortunes, it is true, but not because their real estate portfolios were unwisely chosen. They failed because each went out and borrowed too much money to support their huge and unwieldy purchases.

We needn't look at billionaires to see the potential for disaster in real estate dealing; let's look at the fellow next door. He gathers together $100,000 and purchases a $400,000 property. Fair enough. But then the market abruptly drops

25% (as it did back in the late 1980s in much of Canada), and the man's equity has been wiped out.

Suddenly, it is the bank, which holds $300,000 in equity, that gives the man a "margin call," insisting that he puts up more money on the now-lower-priced property. The man fails to come up with the cash, so he loses the building to the bank. The latter, in turn, dumps it on the open market for little more than $200,000, which only exacerbates the crashing real estate prices in the city, and the snowball of Real Estate Crash gathers speed and size as it rolls down the hill.

But to allow that unfortunate fellow next door — or the ugly collapse of the Campeau and Reichmann fortunes — to allow you to be turned off the concept of purchasing a good real estate portfolio is as absurd (and as self-defeating) as allowing a cousin's loss of his life savings on a Vancouver Stock Exchange "hot tip" to turn you away from investing in quality businesses, mutual fund companies, or their best financial products.

When one buys into a respectable REIT, as many wealthy people do, the property is paid for; there is no mortgage against it; it has good tenants; and every month all one receives is good income — not threatening faxes from a bank. These real estate income trusts are private, it's true, but many are available on the open market, in which both developers and investors have put together a portfolio consisting of solid properties.

One should be careful not to be scared away from the word "trust," which we often identify, if only subconsciously, with the greasy used-car dealer who whispers to us, "*You can trust me* about this fine automobile!"

Mutual funds are, in fact, trust units. (In England, that is

exactly what they are called.) All "trust" means is that someone has a mandate to set up a vehicle for investment. So, for
example, the mandate for a well-managed mutual fund
should be to purchase the common stocks of excellent businesses and hold them indefinitely with no price target or
time frame. The mandate of, say, REITs is to buy income-
producing malls and office buildings. And the mandate of a
Royalty Trust like, for example, the NCE Petrofund, is to buy
producing oil and gas properties. They are all, ultimately, the
same, and they are all trusts.

So What Is with These New Royalty Trusts?

Royalty Trusts, such as the NCE Petrofund I, are further
examples of the most attractive ways to earn income in a
tax-friendly manner. You receive oil and gas income through
your unit trusts, and you pay the government very little until
you sell them — just like your Systematic Withdrawal Plans.
Only Alberta offers this, but you can buy them anywhere in
Canada, and claim the Alberta Royalty Tax Credit. It is a reliable and tax-preferred new investment vehicle available in
this country, and I recommend it highly to my clients.

A good description of these so-called Royalty Trusts was
given recently by chartered accountant Tim Cestnick: "A
royalty trust is a new type of investment that can provide a
healthy stream of income (royalties), often without tax until
a future year." And, he notes, these tax shelters are *not* risky,
not expensive, provide good tax flow, and do not "offend"
Revenue Canada — all problems inherent in other kinds
of shelters.

What I like about Royalty Trusts such as NCE Petrofund

I is that individual investors can capture the benefits of regular cash flow, increased purchasing power, and professional management — all things that are usually reserved for petroleum industry experts and large financial institutions. And by acquiring Royalty interests in existing oil and gas properties that have proven reserves and a history of production, this petrofund has proven itself to be an attractive, conservative oil and gas investment.

Note my use of the word "conservative." Purchasing a Royalty Trust such as NCE's is *not* the same as buying the stock in an oil company — and this is crucial. Since NCE Petrofund I is an investment trust, net income is taxed only at the unit holder level. But oil companies must pay taxes at the corporate level, and any dividends paid are further taxed in the hands of the shareholder! As I keep noting throughout this book, our governments are our partners, but why should we make them our masters?

You already can see the advantage. And if the above paragraph is not attractive enough to you, please recall that most oil companies, by their very nature, are always engaging in exploration, refining, and marketing. A good Royalty Trust, by investing only in producing properties, avoids such major administrative and overhead costs.

Throughout this book I have stressed my passionate belief and faith in long-term investing. Which is another reason why I find Royalty Trusts such excellent investment opportunities: they are traditionally viewed as long-term. Still, for those who are concerned about liquidity, many of these trusts, such as the NCE Petrofund I, are listed and traded on the Toronto Stock Exchange — and are eligible investments for RRSPs, as well.

In all of these cases, one of the key points of this book keeps re-emerging: if you hold on to an investment, be it common shares, mutual funds, REITs, or Royalty Trusts (and/or withdraw your profits from it on a regular basis), there is little or no tax to pay. When you don't sell something, capital gains tax becomes *no* tax.

But What if That Dreaded Market Correction Occurs?

Once again, fear raises its ugly head, and we all know what President Roosevelt said about it, back in the dark days of the Second World War: fear is the only thing we should ever fear.

So the market suffers a severe "correction" (as it's done dozens of times over this century, as I pointed out in an earlier chapter). So countless stocks and mutual funds take a severe hit, and drop (seemingly) precipitously. This does not mean that one should alter one's Systematic Withdrawal Plan, any more than it means that one should call one's broker and scream "Sell!"

Ignore the stock market down-turn. *Ignore* the antichrists and nay-sayers of the newspapers and magazines. *Continue* your Systematic Withdrawal Plan and stop checking the scoreboard, because the value of your mutual funds and the value of your stocks and the value of your financial portfolio will turn around and come back — they always have and they always will.

The truth of the above paragraph is dependent upon several salient points, however: that you have not been diversifying wildly (by spreading your money into a half-dozen funds or more, like so many financial planners foolishly suggest — "Diversification is protection against ignorance," declared Warren Buffett). That you have been avoiding the latest "hot" mutual fund or get-rich-quick penny-stock tips. And that you have been investing — *long-term* investing — in quality mutual funds such as the ones whose remarkable records I have noted in this chapter, such as Trimark or Templeton. Or AIC funds or the new Infinity family, for example, all of which put their money into superior businesses with decades-long brilliant track records, such as Coca-Cola, Gillette, and, yes, Berkshire Hathaway, Mr. Buffett's holding company.

A portfolio consisting of rock-solid businesses and mutual funds can *never* become worthless (which is every investor's worst nightmare) because it simply cannot happen. Your Systematic Withdrawal Plan should continue to redeem money for you regularly, and your high-quality financial portfolio will continue to grow, as the stock markets of the world will inevitably march onward and upward — as they always have.

Still not sold on buying (quality) common stocks and mutual funds, rather than "risk-free" investments such as Guaranteed Investment Certificates, and United States and Canada Savings Bonds? Read the next chapter and smile. (Or weep, if you've traditionally gone the "guaranteed" way.)

14

Concentrate,
Don't Diversify

THE famous quotation goes that "there are lies, damned lies, and statistics." But statistics often tell profound truths, as do charts. And charts of the way stock markets move, and the way successful stocks move, can be very informative, indeed.

The headline on the front page of the November 29, 1996, *Globe and Mail* Report on Business section read "TSE Shatters 6,000," with a chart right below it, covering the years 1970 to the present. I needn't reproduce it for you to be able to declare that it's no straight line, but rather a lot of jagged edges.

So, while the Toronto Stock Exchange composite index of 300 stocks was at 1,012 in 1977, just 36 months later it broke 2,000. Another 74 months later, in March of 1986, it broke 3,000; 16 months later (in July 1987), it moved past 4,000. It took another 102 months — until February of 1996

— to make it to 5,000, and then only 10 more months to reach the latest "magical" number of 6,000.

Over that same period of a quarter-century-plus, there were several recessions (in 1970, 1974, 1979, 1981–82, and 1989 91), as well as a rather diverse collection of prime ministers who "ran" this country, building up deficits and playing with interest rates through the Bank of Canada: Pierre Trudeau. Joe Clark. Trudeau again. John Turner, quickly followed by Brian Mulroney. Kim Campbell, rapidly replaced by Jean Chrétien. In the United States, they saw the presidencies of Nixon, Ford, Carter, Reagan, Bush, and Clinton.

Yet throughout all the recessions, all the procession of political leaders, the composite index of 300 stocks on the TSE zigged and zagged its way up that huge, steep mountain. The zigs are applauded by everyone, of course, but the zags often scare the hell out of investors — and you've seen in this book how low my opinion of "fear" is when it comes to intelligent investing. Fear is its enemy and destroyer.

Here's my favourite "milestone" in that inexorable climb of the TSE to its record height of 6,000 in late November 1996, as recorded by journalists Angela Barnes and Diana Clifford in *The Globe and Mail*: "July 15, 1996: The composite gets caught up in the sell-off in the United States and loses 86 points, dropping to 4,955. The Dow Jones Industrial Average in New York slumps 161 points to 5,350 in what market analysts are sure is the start of the long awaited correction. History proves otherwise."

The market analysts were "sure" — and *I'm* sure that thousands of brokers phoned tens of thousands of their clients that afternoon to beg them to sell, while happily gobbling up their commissions on each sale. But they were wrong. And they were fearful. And that single day — July 15, 1996 — was arguably the best day to purchase quality stocks and mutual funds at a "good," or at least lower, price that entire record-setting year.

I have always felt that the vast majority of people set up their investments lacking the correct, positive attitude of "investing to become wealthy." They do quite the opposite, in fact: they set up their financial portfolios out of fear of losing their money!

So what do they do? They buy bonds. They buy GICs. They buy Canada and U.S. Savings Bonds. They buy all of these "guaranteed" investment vehicles that, in fact, have *very little true growth potential*. Alas, the stock broker or investment advisor who is setting up that portfolio with that nervous negative client doesn't want to lose him, much less get sued. So he invariably creates a portfolio with a huge diversification, and very little concentration.

Most portfolios are far too diversified. Isn't it interesting that wealthy people rarely have much, if any, diversification in their financial ownership? Indeed, the majority of the super-rich have their money sunk into one business. Think of Frank Stronach, who does not put his money in dozens of different companies; he owns a company called Magna, since he buys and holds his own firm, has faith in it, and puts his money where his mouth and his time and his soul are.

The same can be said of Ken Thomson (with his Canadian newspapers, his legal publishing firm, The Bay department stores) and Bill Gates (Microsoft), and, of course, Warren Buffett (Berkshire Hathaway). As the latter writes in his annual report, "we eat our own cooking." And wouldn't you rather feast in a fine restaurant where the chef cannot wait

167

to sit down to a meal he has prepared himself, than in an eatery where the cook sends out for a pizza?

It is not only individual investors like you and me who tend to over-diversify; so do far too many "managers" of mutual funds. No point in being a hero and risking everything, they seem to be saying. Let's buy stocks — lots and lots of stocks — and hope that at least a *few* turn out to be winners. Indeed, the traditional mutual fund holds three, four, even five dozen stocks and more, always diversifying to cover their assets (vulgar pun intended).

GICs and CSBs Are *Not* Good Investments

During the same week that the TSE composite shot past 6,000, I heard on Canadian radio some pretty amazing declarations, and then read similar thoughts in some daily newspapers that forced me to accept that my ears weren't lying to me.

Here is essentially what some experts declared, in my own paraphrase: "You know, you're actually doing better today with your GIC, which millions purchase in order to obtain 'regular' income! Back in the early 1980s, when Canada Savings Bonds paid 19% and GICs were around 15%, inflation was around 12%, so your after-tax return was infinitesimal; you really weren't making any money at all. But today (you lucky kid, you), inflation is only 1% and we're paying you around 3% on your GIC, so after taxes, you're making nearly 1% a year! You're doing so much better!"

Can you *believe* this? It reminds me of what a nutritionist once wrote about white bread that brags that it's "fortified with over 30 vitamins!" Sure, the health food advocate declared, those bakers are showing sensitivity to your health by putting all those vitamins into their bread. What they never tell you is that they refine all the nutrients out of the flour before they bake it, so that it loses nearly all of its value; only then do they put in the vitamins. Should we thank the bakers for putting back in the vitamins they had removed?

The banks apparently think that we should thank them! Let's think back to those magnificent Canada Savings Bonds that the banks eagerly flogged to their unsuspecting customers in the early 1980s. Ottawa actually offered 19.5% in interest on CSBs that year, and the citizens of this great land were so impressed with this astonishingly high rate that the government had to actually put a limit on how much each person could buy! (I think it was around $15,000, but who cares?)

Was this as good a deal as it sounded at the time?

Quite the opposite. If you adjust that rate for taxes and inflation — let's say you are in the 50% bracket — that glorious 19.5% interest now drops by half to only 9.75%. And since inflation that terrible year was a towering 12.5%, all that those wonderful CSBs "with the great rates!" accomplished for you was a loss of over 3% that year.

A loss of 3%! On a hundred thousand bucks invested in Canada Savings Bonds that year — assuming that you were "lucky" enough to buy that high an amount! — you *lost* $3,000. Gee, you could have probably done better with the slot machines down in Vegas. So much for those thrilling interest rates of yesteryear! So much for the way most people felt it was "wonderful to buy a savings bond!" that year.

No, it's not fraud. But it sure is stupidity. It was simply an ugly case of the government of Canada needing the public to finance the bad management of their monetary affairs. A government touting savings bonds is really no different than a person overspending each month and then going to his bank and exclaiming, "I overspent, and I really need to borrow some money to make my mortgage payment!" It was simply bad behaviour on the government's part, since if it ever learned to live within its means, it would not need to borrow from the public, which is precisely what savings bonds are all about: big governments — whether Ottawa, Washington, or London — borrowing money from Peter to pay for Paul's dreadful spending habits. Brilliant. Simply brilliant.

And the government of Canada has not really acted with any more honesty ever since — and the banks have continued to flog their dreadful, dog-food product. So, if you purchased Canada Savings bonds (series 42) in 1987, you earned 9% that year, 10.16% the following year, and a whopping 10.91% the following year, followed by 10.75% the next. But how about the years after that? Well, in 1991, your interest rate on S42 bonds dropped to 7.5%, then to 6% in 1992, and only 5.125% in 1993. Figure in the income tax on that, and the inflation rates of those same years (which drifted between 4% and 5.6% through 1991, before it finally fell below 2% in 1992), and you can see how lousy you did. If you made any money at all!

I could do the same with year after year of CSBs, but let me just jump to November 1996 and their latest series, S51: That series of bonds promised 3% for the last two months of that year, then a "leap" to 4% for 1997, 5% in 1998, 6% in 1999, and a giant 6.5% in 2000. Once again, if you figure in taxes and even a presumably low interest rate, you are making only pennies on this so-called trustworthy savings vehicle.

"Risky" Bank Stocks or "Guaranteed" Investments?

Many years ago, there used to be a common warning to young women who chose to move in with their boyfriends without the latter making a commitment to marriage. It was a bit crude, but had a lot of truth in it: "Why should he buy the cow when the milk is free?" (In other words, why should this guy ever marry you? He's getting what he wants without the promise, the engagement ring, the wedding!)

I thought of that old expression (which is probably still used, along with a wagging finger, by many a parent to their daughters today) because it echoed in my mind when I thought of the absurdity of anyone purchasing Guaranteed Investment Certificates over the stock of the bank that issues these horrible financial vehicles: "Why buy the milk from a bad investment, when you can get the cow that *offers* it?"

The milk, in this case, is those lousy GICs that so many Canadians have counted on for "guaranteed," "regular," and "risk-free" income, and the magnificent, handsome, pedigree cows (i.e., banks) that are forever increasing in value, making huge profits, and paying excellent dividends to the owners of their common shares.

I could give you dozens of examples, but here are just a few.

In 1982, you could have purchased a GIC from your friendly neighbourhood Toronto Dominion branch, and received a whopping 14% interest! (Of course, the inflation rate was nearly 11% that year in Canada, but they never remind you of that; so with taxes and inflation, you actually lost money over those 12 months.)

Or, that same year, you could have taken the same money that you could have put into that TD GIC and purchased that bank's common shares on the Toronto Stock Exchange instead. The price? $6.63 per share.

The price of each share exactly 12 months later? Way up to $8.25 — an increase of over 20% — and that doesn't include the dividends paid that year from the bank on each share of its common stock.

I should mention that the price of a single share of Toronto Dominion Bank on the TSE broke $20 in 1993, reached $24 by 1995, and as of late November 1996 had reached $37. And by June 1997, $41.

Of course, you could always buy a GIC from TD in 1996, while its stock price was shooting up over 50% that year, and get a rate of 3%, if so desired. But why desire that rotten deal at all?

Let's have some similar fun with the Bank of Montreal, shall we? In 1984, you could have purchased some GICs from that fine bank and received a generous 10.5%; not bad, you thought to yourself. Of course, the shares of that bank — so risky, being the stock market, as we all know so well — were going for $12.75 each. (Oh, yes — inflation that year was down to below 5%. Lucky you.)

One year later, you may choose to cash in your safe, "guaranteed" GIC, and get that wonderful 10%+ interest, losing only half to inflation, and another half, if not more, to income tax. Or you could check your stock market prices and discover that those shares of Bank of Montreal going for

$12.75 in 1984 were now up to $17.25 — over 33% higher than a year earlier. Were you crazy?

Let's do one more bank; if this doesn't win you over, what will? Let's choose the year 1989 this time. You take out a GIC from the Royal Bank, Canada's largest and often most success-ful financial institution, and you get nearly 11% interest on it. Fabulous — if you ignore the 5% inflation rate that year.

Of course, you could have bought shares in the same bank offering you that GIC on the Toronto Stock Exchange; they would have cost you $25 each. Today, in mid-1997, you can always renew that great GIC and receive nearly 3% interest on it. Meanwhile, the shares of Royal Bank stock have done slightly better — they broke $50 in late November 1996 and $60 in June of 1997, up rather pleasingly from $31.13 a share at the end of 1995.

And please don't forget that every one of the major banks of Canada have not only seen their common shares zooming upward over the past several years but are regularly offering dividends on each share as well — leaving the miserable rates on each bank's GICs in the dust and far behind. Zooming upward? More like blasting off.

Here are some more numbers to savour. In 1979, you could buy shares of Bank of Nova Scotia from a broker for $8.13 a share; in late 1996, the price of each share pushed past $46. (In June 1997, Nova Scotia moved about $60.) In those same two years, you could buy common shares of the Bank of Commerce for $12.81 and $61.10, respectively.

What have I been showing you? That everyone — from teenagers to Generation Xers to Baby Boomers to retirees — should never buy term deposits or T-bills or Canada Savings Bonds or GICs offered by their local bank; they should be investing in banks. Buy bank stocks — not their crummy products. That's where the money is. Buy the cow itself, not the sour milk they are forever pushing you to purchase.

Here's my point, captured in a single, stunning example. On November 25, 1996, you could have purchased a GIC from any of Canada's Top Five banks and got something like 3% interest — probably a bit less.

Yet on that same day every one of those giant banks saw its common stock go up an average of 3%. (The Bank of Montreal's stock jumped $1.80 per share, to $44.65; Royal's shares went up $2.10, to $48.75; Toronto Dominion leapt $1.70, to $36.20; the Bank of Nova Scotia moved up $1.50, to hit $46.05; Canadian Imperial Bank of Commerce shot ahead $1.85, to reach $59.10.)

There you have it: 3% a year on their GICs, or 3% in a single day with every one of their common stocks.

Is there really a choice here?

Two Very Telling Letters from the Not-So-Distant Past

I recently came across two quite extraordinary letters that were exchanged between a very typical Canadian citizen and a typical Canadian bank. And this was not so long ago, the fall of 1983. I shall leave the names off "to protect the innocent," but I believe that this dialogue captures both pithily and painfully what I have been saying over the last few pages.

Bank of Montreal
Shareholders Services Division
First Canadian Place
Toronto, Ontario

Dear Mr. _____,

In 1952 my father retired from farming and had a house and roughly $100,000. He invested in Canada Savings Bonds and similar investments. Mother is still living and she has made similar investments.

Now instead of this type of investments, had Father bought $100,000 worth of Bank of Montreal shares, we would obviously be better off today. Can you tell me how many shares we would have today? If you can give me the dividend history over that period it would be appreciated. I personally have 1,600 common shares of Bank of Montreal and 500 of your preferred stock.

Your help regarding the above would be most appreciated.

And here is the reply to that letter:

Dear Mr. _____:

In 1952, your father could have acquired roughly 3,400 shares, which, after a five-for-one split in 1967, would be 17,000 shares today, with a current market value of $456,875 (at the $26.875 close of business price, October 20, 1983). In computing this value, we have not taken into consideration a further $410,093 of dividends that would have been earned since that time. Unfortunately, we do not have any way of reflecting your father's individual tax position so we cannot determine how many shares he might have bought out of his net dividends.

I hope this is helpful to you.

How's that for an interesting statement about the advantages of purchasing the common shares of banks, rather than their GICs?

Sometimes I think of banks in the same way that I think of tobacco companies: they hook you when young, and you become emotionally, if not physically, addicted to them. In the case of the latter, you know what I'm talking about. Smoking is "cool." The guy with the cigarette gets the girl, or at the very least lassoes the horse. And Joe Camel is such a cute cartoon character, isn't he?

Look at what banks do: they flood the grade schools with colouring books; they fill every parent's mind with the belief that if you don't teach your kids to put their birthday money into a savings account (paying $\frac{1}{2}$%, maybe 1% if you're really fortunate), then you are an abusive mummy or daddy.

So we all get hooked on banks and banking and banking products. And then they have us for life, to purchase blindly their products and services, while making their shareholders wealthy instead of us!

No, banks don't cause cancer or heart disease or emphysema. But if the public continues to buy that line about "you're far safer with a CSB/GIC," then they are only asking to end up as "refugees," hammering on the doors of their financial planners, begging them to help them out. Their GIC, which paid them 5.5% back in 1994, just came due, and they can't even get 3% on the renewal! Their earnings have just dropped around 50%, and they can't make ends meet! What should they do?

What should they do? Read over this chapter — and buy bank stocks. Those are the real cash cows.

Are RRSPs the Best Way to Go?

Every January and February of each year, Canadians probably see the letters "RRSP" more frequently than the words "McDonald's" or "Donuts." (In the U.S., it's IRAs.) And we all know why. In those two months, tens of billions of dollars are poured into Registered Retirement Savings Plans, out of the fervent — if not necessarily realistic — hope that a few thousand dollars tucked away each winter (tax free!) will eventually amount to enough for them and their spouses to live on after retirement.

Now, there is nothing *wrong* with RRSPs, except I'd like to make a brief argument here that there isn't much *right* with them, either. Indeed, a very strong argument can be made for leveraging — in other words, borrowing — to invest on your own, rather than socking away a few grand annually into an RRSP.

In order to do this clearly, I'd like to set up two straw men: Person A, who puts a $12,000 contribution into his RRSP, and Person B, who borrows $150,000 from a bank at 5% (or 8%, or whatever the rate is at the time). Let's first discuss what these two men and their two investment plans have in common.

Person A's $12,000 RRSP contribution is a kind of forced savings; so is Person B's borrowing the 150 grand from his bank, at least in this case.

Person A's $12,000 has a tax deferral, of course; that's much of the charm and value of RRSPs. But Person B actually can write off that $150,000 loan as a tax deduction, not unlike the way that Americans may deduct their mortgage payments on their houses.

Finally, both Person A and Person B have one thing perfectly in common: each of their investments will now
undergo tax-free compounding.

Okay, so what are the pitfalls of Person A's RRSP contribution, and what are the benefits of Person B's $150,000
bank loan? You may find some of them surprising. Here's the
first one: Person A must put a minimum of 80% of his RRSP
contribution each year into Canadian stocks and bonds —
that's four-fifths (!) into a country that handles but *2%* of the
world's trading in commodities! (There's nothing wrong with
investing in one's country — but 80 cents of every dollar?)

Not so with Person B, who is free to invest *all 100%* of
his loan anywhere in this very exciting globe: China, Japan,
England, South Africa, Israel, South America — anywhere.
I feel that this fellow has the real benefit in this case.

Here's another important difference between our two
men: the RRSP of Person A has absolutely *zero collateral
value*. If he wishes to borrow to invest in a business, or for
any reason, whether he has $10 or $10 million in his RRSP, it
is simply valueless as collateral. And Person B? His $150,000
has *full collateral value*, which could prove crucial at any
point in his lengthy business or family life.

Here's one that may really throw you: when Person A
eventually begins to withdraw his RRSP, *every penny will
be 100% taxable*. Not so with Person B, who took out the
loan. The return of his principal is tax-free, and when he
makes a profit — which he undoubtedly will, if he follows the
suggestions made in this book! — his capital gains are only
75% taxable. So, if he withdraws, say, $20,000 in capital
gains, he will pay taxes on only $15,000. Quite an advantage
over his RRSP-loving friend, Person A.

Other pitfalls for the more-travelled route of Person A and his RRSP are more obvious: RRSPs are government-controlled, of course, while Person B has the benefit of having no government controlling anything he does with his money.

And there are maximum contribution limits for any RRSP, which are always changing, but still always limited to a small percentage of a person's annual earnings. Not so with Person B, who has no maximum limits whatsoever on the amount that he chooses to borrow from the bank and invest anywhere in the world.

Another pitfall for Person A is that, should he choose at any time to borrow to invest in his RRSP, the interest on that loan is not tax-deductible. Yet it is quite the opposite for Person B, whose interest on his loan is fully tax-deductible — as are all investment loans.

Furthermore, RRSPs assume that Canadians will be in a lower tax bracket when they retire — something that is hardly true for most of us, especially those who have invested well. But Person B's plan allows him, and all Canadians who choose to go his way, to plan for a retirement lifestyle that they can look forward to.

Finally, Person A's RRSP route — surely the road most frequently travelled by Canadians — has but a small capital amount working for him, which is a definite pitfall. But Person B, with his tax-deductible bank loan of $150,000, has a large capital amount working for him, and one that can do brilliantly when not limited to Canadian purchases, has full collateral value, is only 75% taxable on its capital gains, is not government-controlled, has no contribution limits, and has its interest tax-deductible.

The winner? As they announce at boxing matches, I suggest that it is clearly Person B (and by a knock-out) with his bank loan, over Person A, with his small annual contributions into his RRSP. Remember, I'm not saying that RRSPs are worthless or harmful. But I am suggesting that leveraging oneself (see the Laws of Wealth, above) is always the way to go in order to guarantee a comfortable, even lavish, retirement — and not the much-touted RRSP. I want to challenge the conventional wisdom here, and put it as clearly as I can: RRSP contributions are simply not sufficient for your future happiness and financial security.

15

Seek Out a Full-Service
Financial Advisor

MY partner David Singh uses the analogy of a sports team
to dramatize the importance of the relationship one has
to one's investment advisor. There are three components to a
great team: the players, the coaching staff, and the owner. The
successful investor is like the owner, who really just sits back
and enjoys profits and the increase in value that comes over
time from the efforts of the coaching staff (the investment
advisor) with the players (the mutual funds and stocks, etc.).

In choosing this all-important investment advisor, you
need to find someone who has a very profound philosophy
about how money should be managed. I firmly believe that
the success of any investment will come from two primary
sources: the *quality of investment* made on behalf of the
investor (whether it be mutual funds or in a single business,
through the purchase of common stock) and *the duration
of time* that it is held.

I have often mentioned in these pages the awesome story of Coca-Cola, that a $40 investment made in 1919 would have been worth close to $6 million in the summer of 1997. It is clear from that single company's history that the root of all wealth lies in ownership of an excellent business, and the indefinite time period it is owned.

I must be vulgar here, for emphasis: most financial portfolios are structured for mediocrity, since the majority of investment advisors are simply protecting their asses! And if they are recommending mutual funds, then the managers of those funds are also protecting their own asses.

In the case of most brokers, if you say that you wish to put $100,000 into a portfolio of stocks, most will recommend between five and ten companies. The average mutual funds salesperson will recommend a half-dozen mutual funds — and each one of them has dozens of stocks in its possession! So you end up owning many hundreds of stocks, which only guarantees that your portfolio will be far too over-diversified to bring in any good returns. This over-diversification only guarantees mediocrity.

If your investment advisor has no real philosophy, he will sell you what Mr. Warren Buffett calls "the Noah style of investment" — two of these, two of those, two of them, and so on. This occurs because there is no serious belief in anything.

Real growth, as I keep noting, is generated by investing in a few solid investments, not dozens or hundreds. Mr. Buffett made another good comment on this question that is worth noting: in a lifetime of investing, if you were given only 20 good ideas, and if every time you use one of them you have to punch a card (leaving 19, then 18, and so on), you would be a lot more careful and thoughtful about how to allocate your investment capital. This is because you would know that you had only a limited amount of opportunity in your lifetime and would therefore be a lot less reluctant to simply blunder along. This is a good attitude to have.

Most money managers or mutual fund managers don't add much value, because of their foolish use of such questionable concepts as sector rotation, asset allocation, thematic investing, and so on. Those are all the styles of someone who is guessing, speculating, reckless, and highly unreliable.

So where does the "cover your ass" problem arise? It is always present when you have mutual funds managers who have no incentive to do anything special for their investors because they want to keep their jobs. In 1996, there was a prominent manager of a major mutual fund company in the United States who decided to do something "special." He suddenly withdrew most of the tens of millions his fund had invested in stocks and placed it heavily into bonds. The value of the bonds went down while stock prices shot up, leading to mediocre returns for a mutual fund that had been a stellar performer to this point. He was unceremoniously fired.

Of course, when a mutual funds manager makes a recommendation and tries to do something special that really works well, he gets a pat on his back and gets to keep his job. But this is no way for you, as an investor with valid hopes and dreams, to steadily grow your portfolio through consistent, philosophically based purchases.

In brief, everyone is covering his or her respective asses, by over-diversifying, or by going with the latest "special" trend or fad.

A further dilemma arises from investment advisors who try to sell mutual funds by their past performance. ("Look! The XYZ Fund shot up 28% last year! It's got a great track record!") Now, with a quality stock of a great company such as a Coca-Cola or a Microsoft or a major bank, there could well be some truth in that suggestion. But when talking about mutual funds, there is hardly any relevance to such a statement.

Why? Well, I know one very major mutual fund that bought and sold some 600 different common stocks during 1995! Indeed, many mutual funds don't have the same stocks in their portfolios only two weeks after they buy them. So how can any mutual fund dealer try to sell a particular fund only on its past performance when the contents of that fund are very often greatly changed?

So here's a powerful statement for you to consider: if someone tries to sell you on purchasing a mutual fund *solely* on its past performance, he or she is selling you a lie.

As I've noted often throughout this book, all wealth is created by taking intelligent risk. But if you believe that you can avoid risk by buying bonds, you are sadly mistaken. Bonds, please remember, have a minimum floor, all right, but they also have a maximum ceiling. With the ownership of a good business (through the purchase of its common stock), however, there is neither a floor nor a ceiling. True, that lack of a floor in terms of its value can be off-putting to many. But with a magnificent stock like, say, Gillette, that floor is never too low, whereas its ceiling can rise forever.

Here's an ugly bond story, and it has to do with a company whose products we have all loved since our youth. Walt Disney did a horrible thing to a group of bondholders a few years ago, when it borrowed $50 million to make the animated motion picture *The Lion King*.

The eventual profits, as you may be aware, from the sale of movie tickets, books, the video, plush toys, and countless other merchandising spin-offs, has already surpassed, by the middle of 1997, $1 billion — and counting.

So what was the terrible thing that this grand company did to those bondholders? It merely paid them back their $50 million, plus a small interest on the loan.

They received no free movie passes. They obtained no free T-shirts — nor any profit on the hundreds of thousands sold. They got no free CDs of the great soundtrack. They were handed no complimentary videos for their kids. Nor were they invited to the annual meeting of the company.

The holders of those bonds received nothing but an insultingly small interest on their loan, because *bondholders own nothing*! True, there was a floor on their investment, so they could never "lose it all." But there was a very claustrophobic ceiling. So while they made their 6, 7, or 8% on their loan to Walt Disney, those who had been wise enough to purchase common shares in the company more than doubled their money over the same period of time. Not too smart. But then, the enormous, stunning profits of *The Lion King* belonged only to shareholders of Walt Disney stock, and nobody else.

As you can see, choosing a good investment advisor is not easy. But it's a lot less hard when you know to look for one with a solid philosophy of investment; a philosophy that argues that stocks are parts of businesses, that they want to create value for you by helping you to own those businesses for generations — not till just next week or next month or even next year.

Here's the real catch: you must find an investment advisor who will help you to do the things that you *should* do — not the things that you *want* to do. Let me explain. The natural tendencies of the vast majority of us are usually antagonistic to wealth creation, whether due to our desire to get rich quick or to take profits and run. So, what we want to do and what we should do are not necessarily the same.

Think about it. Over the past 65 years, the Dow Jones Industrial Average has gone from 40 to over well over 7,000. More wealth has been created for a generation of North Americans than at any time in history, yet most of that money came into the market only over the past three years. (Those high interest rates, which have been declining steadily over the past two decades, pauperized a generation who were fearful of investing; they were thrilled to get 12% or more at their neighbourhood bank.) So, most people are suicidal with their own, macho tendencies towards investment — invariably, they want to buy high and sell low, often without even knowing it.

I can assure you of several constants. Declines in the market and in stock prices are a certainty, all right — but they are invariably temporary. It is the advances that are permanent; they are the only things that are truly lasting. Over the long-term, the stock market will deliver superior returns.

The job of the good investment advisor, then, is to help you enjoy every day of those wonderful, marvellous advances in the stock market. There's a price tag, of course, and that is that you must stay with all the declines, as well as with the advances. But I swear to you, *this is not too high a price to pay*!

Of course, it takes courage to hold your course, because markets are cyclical and can be unpredictable, even absurd. There are those inevitable corrections, which scare the hell out of 90% of people, who panic and sell their shares — leaving wise men and women like you to look at this (brief) bear market and see a flashing neon sign that reads *THE BIG SALE IS ON! BUY NOW!!* Which is when you should be buying even more common shares of fine businesses than ever before.

You need an investment advisor who will help you put together an investment program and then *keep* it together, against your natural, self-destructive tendencies. Because if you leave the market during its (inevitable) declines, you will miss the opportunities for that inevitable market rise. And then, if the market rises when you are out of it, you might not want to get back in again.

So you have to stay invested! Find an investment advisor who will help you to "turn off" the stock market and focus on the playing field — not the scoreboard. To help you realize that even if we are in an economic slump, or the province of Quebec is threatening separation, or there are riots on the streets of American cities, or war in the Balkans, these have nothing to do with your being a part-owner of some of the world's great businesses — businesses that will continue to produce great earnings over time.

Your investment advisor should really be more of a coach, someone who has your well-being and your best interests at heart. And these interests should include everything from wealth creation, to multi-generational wealth creation, especially estate planning, wills, transferring assets to the second generation, making sure that you can take care of your parents in the best possible fashion, educate your grandchildren, and much more.

You don't necessarily want an investment advisor to educate you; you have done that by reading this book. You need one who will have the trust and faith to help you to keep investing in, and holding, great common stock. To help you keep your fears at bay. To agree with you that the market is not an end in itself, but a means to an end — to achieve your financial goals and dreams, and those of your descendants. (And don't forget what I've noted earlier: 30 years ago, when someone retired, they could expect only another eight years of life; today, a retiree can look forward to another quarter-century on this earth. All the more time to see great stocks increase in value; all the more time that you will need successful investments to pay your bills.)

The quality investment advisor should be concerned with all of these things — and not merely to pick up a commission cheque. Which is why the eventual financial advisor you choose to work with should have a profound, sincere, steady, *proven* investment philosophy — like the one I have been espousing throughout this book.

Invest and grow rich. My title says it all.

Conclusion

Imagine that in some private business you own a small share
that cost you $1,000. One of your partners, named Mr. Market, is
very obliging indeed. Every day he tells you what he thinks your
interest is worth and furthermore, offers either to buy you out or
sell you an additional interest on that basis. Sometimes his idea of
value appears plausible; often, on the other hand, Mr. Market lets
his enthusiasm or his fears run away with him, and the value he
proposes seems to you a little short of silly.

BENJAMIN GRAHAM, in the 1950s

I am not in the business of predicting general stock market
or business fluctuations. If you think I can do this, or think it is
essential to an investment program, you should not be in the
partnership.

WARREN BUFFETT, early in his partnership, in the 1950s

Now, who could argue with the great Benjamin Graham and his renowned disciple Warren Buffett?

I hope that this book has convinced you that there is *simply no alternative to investing* in order to build a nest egg. As I've noted, there are only three things that one can do with money: lend it, spend it, or invest in something that has the potential to increase in value over time.

In every corner of the Free World (and more and more, in places like China and Cuba as well, for the passion for capitalism is universal), *wealth has always been created through business ownership* — with the goal of every business to make money for its shareholders, through providing goods and services to a consumer base.

One might joke that there are some alternatives to investing in a business — or, through the purchase of its common stock, in small parts of a business. After all, you can always marry a wealthy man or woman. Or you can choose to be born into (or be adopted by) a rich family. But these seem a bit less likely and more difficult than to invest in the shares of a good company.

There is a saying that I often quote in my seminars: "Whatsoever I believe, will come to pass in my life; therefore, what I must believe, I must expect. And what I expect, I must experience."

I agree. A person who is poor has a poor attitude, and lacks the courage and moral fibre to do what is right. And what is right is to invest wisely and for long periods of time. Men and women who do not invest; who save their money in bank accounts or in GICs or U.S. or Canada Savings Bonds; who don't leave mediocre jobs to start their own businesses and follow their dreams . . . these people fail to act thoughtfully, because they fear failure. And, sadly, that fear will attract the very thing they fear the most: poverty, despair, and a retirement that will be hungry and even frightening.

Do recall what I wrote, many chapters ago, near the start of this book: we are all the custodians of the 60- or 70-year-old man or woman whom we shall someday be. And if we were to meet our future self on the road, and that person asked us why there is no money, we must be sure to be able to avoid the terribly common reply: "I worked all my life, I raised a family, I saved money — but I didn't invest, because I feared that I might lose money." That sort of existence *always* ends up poor.

My conclusion, then, is really the theme of this entire book: Unless you invest, you will be poor. Unless you invest, you will *never* be able to go from fear to infinity. So invest, and invest wisely, and you *will* grow rich.

It's as simple — and as happy (or as sad) as that.

The choice is up to you.

One Woman's
Astonishing Story

MANY readers may have noticed in their daily newspapers a few years ago — the story was picked up across North America — a touching tale of a lonely old woman who left many millions of dollars after she died to a university she never attended, "so women would be better treated than I had been in my career."

It was with great pleasure that I came across a reprint of a fine article about this extraordinary woman — Anne Scheiber — in the April 1997 issue of *Reader's Digest*, which first appeared in the *Washington Post* on December 17, 1995. I have received permission to reproduce this story, written by James K. Glassman, since it captures exquisitely what I have been sharing with you throughout this book: by choosing quality stocks and holding them for the long-term, astounding gains are almost inevitably made.

Here is the article, reprinted in full, which I feel makes

a perfect appendix to this book; my thanks to journalist Glassman for finding the moral to this story, beyond the simple facts of the woman's generosity in her will.

How to Build a Big Nest Egg

When the story came out in the newspapers two years ago [1993], it seemed too good to be true. A little old lady, living alone in a run-down studio apartment, parlays $5,000 out of her savings into a $20-million fortune and leaves almost all of it to a university that had never heard of her. Even better, she has the last laugh on her ex-employer, an outfit that she felt denied her promotions because she was a woman.

But it was all true. The heroine, Anne Scheiber, worked for the U.S. Internal Revenue Service. Despite her law degree, the IRS never promoted her or paid her more than $3,150 a year ($28,000 in today's money). She retired in 1943 and put her money in stocks. Last year Yeshiva University in New York City found that it was the beneficiary of her estate.

The best part of this story is that by following her investment guidelines, you can do almost as well as this little old lady did. Here are the lessons of Anne Scheiber's amazing success:

Start early. Scheiber was 51 when she invested her $5,000 and 101 when she died. Her companies earned profits on their profits over and over, and in the long run, share prices grew along with corporate earnings, as they almost always do.

Stocks need many years for this "miracle of compounding" to work. That's why the single most important factor in stock-market success is time.

If you want to emulate Scheiber, you should begin much earlier — in your 20s or 30s. At an annual growth rate of 12 percent, an investment of $1,000 in stocks today will become about $100,000 in the year 2036. Assume inflation at three to four percent annually, and that $100,000 will be worth about $25,500 in today's dollars. Not bad.

Buy stocks. As an IRS auditor dealing with estates, Scheiber noticed that the very rich tended to own common stock. This was no fluke. Since 1926 the average annual return on stocks in the United States has been 12.2 percent, compared with 5.7 percent for corporate bonds and 3.7 percent for short-term treasury bills.

If Scheiber had invested only in bonds, her $5,000 would have grown to only about $80,000.

In the late 1970s, Scheiber's stockbroker, William Fay of Merrill Lynch & Co., did persuade her to use some of her stock dividends to buy municipal bonds — a sensible move for a woman in her 80s since, in the short term, bonds are less risky than stocks. But this move into bonds probably limited the total value of her portfolio.

Buy and hold. "She just held on to what she bought and rarely sold anything," says Fay of his client. "She believed in these companies. She just stayed with them. She did not care if the market was up or down."

Scheiber's success is dramatic proof of how well a simple buy-and-hold strategy works. In 1953 she bought

500 shares of Schering-Plough Corp., the pharmaceutical company, for about $6,000. And she just held on. Today, through stock splits, those original 500 shares have become 64,000 shares, worth $3.64 million.

Another of her longtime holdings, Coca-Cola Co., increased in value from $28,000 to $720,000 in 15 years. That doesn't even include $62,000 in dividends.

All of her stocks went through rough patches. Fay says there was a time "during the '70s when Schering-Plough lost half its value." But Scheiber didn't sell, and she was amply awarded for her discipline.

Minimize taxes. Scheiber denied the IRS estate taxes at her death by leaving her money to a nonprofit institution. More important, though, she generally avoided capital gains taxes during her life.

It's a pleasant quirk of the U.S. [and Canadian] tax code that taxes on profits aren't owed until you sell an asset.

If you can hold stocks until your retirement, you've created what amounts to an unlimited individual retirement account [IRA — the equivalent to Canada's RRSP]. Non-IRA investors who churn their portfolios, on the other hand, incur not only brokerage commissions but also repeated tax bites that drastically reduce the power of compounding.

Buy quality. Scheiber avoided fads. She bought solid companies with good balance sheets and strong reputations rather than trying to find the next Microsoft in its cradle. "She focused on franchise names," says Fay. Among them: PepsiCo, Exxon, Chrysler, Warner-Lambert.

Scheiber also bought what she knew. "She was drawn to these stocks by their products," Fay says. She understood pharmaceuticals, so she bought Pfizer, Bristol-Myers and Schering-Plough. She loved the movies, so she bought Loews, which owned a chain of theatres. "She had faith in these companies," according to Fay.

Never touch capital. This is the famous admonition of old wealth, and Scheiber followed it to the hilt. She left her Merrill Lynch account alone and reinvested all the dividends and interest.

"She had the mentality," says Fay, "that she had to exist on her small IRS pension and Social Security." But Scheiber went to extremes. "She had few friends," Fay points out. "By our standards she was an unhappy person, totally consumed by her securities accounts and her money." Making millions doesn't require this kind of obsession. Start early, and you may end up like Anne Scheiber — only a lot happier.